THE OFFICIAL
COMPANION
SEASON 5

24: The Official Companion
Season 5

ISBN 1 84576 541 9
ISBN-13 9781845765415

Published by Titan Books,
a division of Titan Publishing Group Ltd
144 Southwark Street
London SE1 0UP

First edition February 2007
10 9 8 7 6 5 4 3 2 1

Acknowledgements
Portions of the Carlos Bernard interview provided by journalist Bryan Cairns. Thank you so much!

The author would like to extend her thanks and undying appreciation to the amazing behind the scenes team at Fox & *24* publicity: Mariana Galvez, Jenny Kay and Virginia King. Again, these books would not be what they are without the generous time of the entire *24* production team especially Howard Gordon, Joel Surnow, Robert Cochran, all the producers, their assistants and every incredible *24* crew and cast member that made time to share their stories with me.

My personal thanks go out again to my fantastic support group of family and friends that are unfailing in encouraging me and making me laugh even when I'm bleary-eyed and incoherent from deadlines. Special thanks to Gordon; the best editors around: Martin, Natalie C, Paul and Cath; my friends Casey, Dina, Joe Z and my cousin Anita. Thank you for being part of my life!

The publishers would like to thank the cast (both past and present) and crew of *24* for all their help with this book. Many thanks also to Virginia King and Rimma Aranovich at Twentieth Century Fox.

What did you think of this book? We love to hear from our readers. Please email us at: **readerfeedback@titanemail.com** or write to us at the above address. You can also visit us at **www.titanbooks.com**

To receive advance information, news, competitions, and exclusive Titan offers online, please register as a member by clicking the "sign up" button on our website: **www.titanbooks.com**

A CIP catalogue record for this title is available from the British Library.

Printed and bound in the USA.

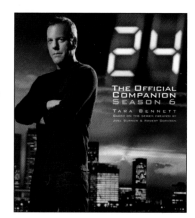

Coming soon...
24: The Official Companion Season 6

THE OFFICIAL COMPANION SEASON 5

TARA DiLULLO BENNETT

TITAN BOOKS

Contents

JACK'S BACK!

Creating Season 5

J ack Bauer is dead. Well, that's what he wants the world to think when he fakes his death at the very end of the fourth season of *24*. And Jack being Jack, even the mission to snuff himself out turned out to be a success. Tired of running from the Chinese, who want to blame him for their Consul's death, and estranged from his family and girlfriend, "perishing" becomes a way for Bauer to shed the horrors of his existence and walk into the sunshine of a new day with a clean slate and an untainted future.

While loyal *24* audiences were immediately panic-stricken about Jack Bauer's fate in the fifth season, their consternation was nothing compared to that of the *24* writers who had to actually figure out how to return Jack Bauer back to his old life. After four years of reinventing their ground-breaking, real-time format, the writers were feeling the pressure to dig deep for new ideas. "I don't underestimate fear and desperation," smiles executive producer and season five showrunner Howard Gordon, contemplating his writing motivations. "Fortunately, the only thing that has changed with experience is panic. I don't panic anymore, which is a good thing. You wind up developing a sense that, with a steady application of effort and an equal measure of faith in your ability, and the abilities of your colleagues to help you, something will happen. It may not always be great, but something good or good enough will happen and sometimes that's just what the doctor ordered."

So, it was in that heightened state of pressurized creativity, known as the "brainstorming stage" for the upcoming season, that the *24* writers/producers gathered to map out how and why Jack Bauer would come back to his life of thwarting terrorism on domestic soil. Executive producer and co-creator Joel Surnow says they initially approached the conundrum pragmatically. "We knew we needed to be within fifteen minutes of Los Angeles, so that was our first thought.

The original idea was that Jack was somewhere around Bakersfield with an assumed name [Frank Flynn]. If he was just a loner and didn't talk to anybody or know anybody you don't have much to play off, so, as part of the necessary elements to make the show go, we thought, 'Let's give him what we call a family.' It's not a real family, but a single woman who is raising her teenage boy seemed like a great place to start." Diane Huxley and her son Derek became Jack's safe harbor, where he stayed as he worked the oilrigs out in the arid landscape of rural California.

Fellow executive producer and co-creator Robert Cochran continues: "We tried to set Jack up so that, in a sense, if he wasn't content, he was temporarily satisfied that he had to live a secret life. A recurring theme of the show is that Jack has a fate that he cannot escape, no matter what he does. Now in this case, he even tried to kill himself to start over and escape his fate." But what would be reason enough for Jack to shed his carefully orchestrated deception and come out of hiding once more?

Howard Gordon admits the team was at a loss until one fateful conversation in the writers' room. "We sat in the room for weeks and we actually had a whole different story that we were working on. We had done weeks of work in a direction that none of us were really excited about and then [co-executive producer] Manny Coto said something like, 'What if Palmer gets shot?' and that really threw that idea into relief. It also asked a lot of questions like, 'Will the audience tolerate his violent death or will it turn people off?' As it evolved, it got even grimmer when Michelle and Tony were going to go down too. It began to feel like the end of *The Godfather* where everybody we loved for all these years is getting knocked off in the first act of season five. We asked ourselves, 'Are we committing suicide here?'"

But the season's storyline immediately coalesced around the powder keg of Palmer's assassination. Cochran explains, "I think two things were involved in the decision to kill Palmer. For four years, we've been through many permutations with his character. He was noble and never completely lost that sense of nobility

by wanting to do the right things. Yet we put him in situations where he had to compromise and face those things. At one point, he resigned from the presidency because he felt he was not able to live up to his own ideals. We had really done a lot with him and there comes a time where you worry that whatever you do next is going to be a repeat in some sense, which is something we try to avoid. One of the reasons we kill characters off is that sometimes we feel like we've gotten to that point that whatever you do will have a familiar ring to it, and we try to keep the show fresh. Secondly, killing Palmer is such a monumental event that it motivates Jack for the rest of the year. It gives him an impetus and a motivation that pries him loose from the relatively comfortable life he was trying to build for himself, and forces him back into the arena, physically and emotionally."

Gordon continues: "Ultimately, it was a bold move that I think sent a message in no uncertain terms to the audience that we were starting with a clean slate.

In some ways it was an answer to what we did with Teri Bauer. Can this show really go to this place? And it did."

Yet it was an idea that didn't sit well with Dennis Haysbert, who took great pride in having created a character that had evolved into an important role model to many. Gordon says he personally broke the news to the actor at a quiet breakfast. "Dennis and I had really developed a close relationship and we still remain really great friends. He had his own reasons for not wanting to portray the death of his character. I told Dennis that, 'Even though he dies physically, I guarantee you that the emotional context of the year will be Jack avenging his death.' I think the pillar of the whole show is really that Jack/Palmer relationship, that upstairs/downstairs relationship. It was the center of the show and so removing one of those pillars was a scary thing. But replacing it with Charles Logan, I think in the end, made for a perfect structure and a very organic place to get to — that the guy that was Palmer's replacement was this terrible villain. So, I told Dennis that, 'Even though you are physically dead, you will be President every single episode.' I also said that we didn't have a story for him. It was a double issue. We had played out Palmer's story and then some. At one point, we actually contemplated having this ex-President strapping on a gun and doing all the things [Dennis] has wound up doing on *The Unit*, but it didn't feel real. I have no regrets. There is nothing more dramatic than a well-earned death. I think it's great to have your story really end and not just peter out."

With Jack's motivation for the season firmly established, the writers moved on to developing the character of Charles Logan (Greg Itzin). Introduced at the end of season four as the weak Vice President, the writers knew they wanted to tell more of his story during season five. Cochran explains: "The original motivation for bringing Charles Logan in at all as a character was that we wanted to bring Dennis Haysbert back. He had resigned as President the year before, so we had to figure out how to get Haysbert back in the show. We had a pretty strong President in Keeler, so we asked, 'What if we kill or disable Keeler? Therefore the burden of government falls on the Vice President and we'll make the VP a weak character. Then somebody can suggest to him that, "It's a tough day, why don't you lean on someone with a little more experience and call

in David Palmer?"' So the whole purpose of Logan was to give us an excuse to call back ex-President Palmer. Well, we looked at the episodes and Itzin was so brilliant as this weasely President!"

Surnow recalls how Itzin's portrayal of Logan really inspired his arc for the season, "Greg was so magnificent that we decided we needed to build a season around this guy. This is a once-in-a-lifetime right actor for the right part. I can't remember seeing a better character on TV than Charles Logan played by this guy. He inhabits him and it's magnificent to watch. So, when you have somebody that good and he's President, we decided to build a whole story around him. Everything we do on *24* is about family, so we gave him a wife, Martha Logan. Jean Smart was our first choice. We wanted someone who was like the woman that cried wolf — someone that everybody thought was crazy, but really was the one who knew what was going on."

Gordon remembers they tried to get Smart in to read, but she was already scheduled with other projects. "She was doing a play or a movie and we couldn't see her for months, so we read a bunch of other people and went down several other paths. But Jean was the first one we thought about and was the one who ended up with the role. From the moment she actually walked into the room, as Joel and I sat there, we couldn't believe how perfect she was. For a character like Charles having a Martha Mitchell-type character, instead of a demure wife, was particularly appealing." Surnow adds, "When you see these two together, it's just magic. Once we saw how well they worked together, we started building on it."

Across the board, the writers were smitten with the onscreen chemistry of Itzin and Smart, whose every troubled interaction just served to feed the storylines. Cochran offers, "The thing that made this season different from other seasons was the stuff between President Logan and Martha Logan. They had a wonderful, twisted relationship in some ways, but the thing that made it riveting was that underneath there was some genuine affection that had gone wrong over the years. They had the pressures of public life and we've all seen that played out many times in politics, so you understand how those things happen. But those two performers were so good. In the same scene they could almost bring tears to your eyes, because you realize there was a love there that wasn't quite working, and then two seconds later, you could be cringing because of what he said to her or she said to him. The flip side of love can be cruelty and almost hatred and they were brilliant at playing the full range of emotions that would be in play in a relationship like that. As writers, we basically kept that going for the whole season and the performers brought something new to each interaction, and I think that's why it felt so fresh."

Surnow concurs, adding, "The Logan story was probably the one season where there was one story other than Jack's that was weighted almost equally. The Palmer story in the first season had a lot going on but it didn't fold into the main story like this one did, so we were able to successfully merge it like it was of a piece. It was a nice stitching."

At the start of the season, the writers didn't know that they would eventually turn Charles Logan into the villain of the year, so they started populating Jack's world with foes to move along his revenge goal. In the first hours of the day, Russian separatists were

introduced to try and thwart Logan's Russian/US terrorist-treaty signing. Executive producer Evan Katz says, "We chose them because we wanted to take a break from the Middle Eastern terror, but they were much less important than the sinister forces behind the nerve gas. Sure you have [separatist leader] Vladimir Bierko [Julian Sands], but he is not as much of a villain as Christopher Henderson [Peter Weller]." Henderson came into the picture mid-day as Jack's former mentor before being revealed as the mastermind behind Palmer's death. "Henderson was conceived as a 'Jack gone wrong'. I don't know if we were aware of how long we'd keep him alive, but he ended up sticking around right up to the very end."

Gordon recalls the evolution of Henderson, "Interestingly, in hindsight, once upon a time he was supposed to be Jack's father. It was an interesting revision. If you look at it, one of our tricks is that we've often gone to these corporate defense contractor guys that have a history with Jack. It's becoming a little bit of a move, but we liked the idea of Jack's mentor being this guy with whom he had this connection as well as a rotten past. We talked about Jack way back in the pilot as being a whistle-blower and to now discover who one of those people might be, and then to discover too that it was Jack's mentor was an intriguing idea."

Meanwhile, Jack also had a lot of personal problems to fix when the news spread inside CTU that he was, in fact, not dead. The women in Jack's life, former girl-friend Audrey Raines (Kim Raver) and his daughter Kim (Elisha Cuthbert) were both brought back to show the emotional repercussions of his decision to "die"; Kim Bauer, particularly, in order to twist the emotional knife for Jack. Katz reflects, "I consider the Audrey part of the story more successful emotionally, but the Kim story worked because we went to such an un-comfortable place with it. It wasn't easily resolved and tied up."

Surnow continues, "We wanted it to be hard. Again, our show lives in the discomfort and not the comfort zone. She has a lot of anger toward her dad when she finds out he was alive, so she played out that emotion. I think that's what makes the show interesting as opposed to it just being tidy and neat and happy."

Kim's continued anger toward Jack is something that has not endeared her to many fans over the years, and Gordon says he finally thinks he understands why: "I think to some degree her character has unfortunately been a reflection of how much people adore Jack Bauer. She was a necessary foil in season one for Jack. In some ways, she was created to make Jack's life harder and I think people have always resented her for it. In season five we brought her back, and once again she's not forgiving Jack, but that was as much to make Jack alone as to make Jack and Audrey front and center as the primary relationship in Jack's life. The character and the actress, unfortunately, have become sacrificial lambs to create that situation, not consciously on our part, but I think that's why the audience responds to her so strongly. I've got to say that Elisha is great! She

couldn't be more loveable or better at what she does, but the part has that challenge."

Reflecting on some of the other major beats of the season, the writers admit some ideas worked better than others. Katz says, "We definitely got backed into some corners. I know that if you take a step back and look at the Russian separatists who do the hijacking, it is extremely complicated and it would take a novel to explain it all. Getting all that narrative to be clear and interesting was hard. We were trying to forge new ground and it gets harder every year because we have covered so much ground. But something that was fortunate was that we picked nerve gas at the beginning of the year. It was a particularly good decision that enabled us to do the mall story where Jack has to prevent the gas being released on people. It also allowed us to kill everyone at CTU, particularly Edgar Stiles [Louis Lombardi], which was an important thing, and it sort of enabled us to set up the end."

As to CTU, Surnow says he enjoyed the various bureaucratic shake-ups they introduced. "Homeland Security came in to take over CTU with a new cast of

characters led by Karen Hayes, played by Jayne Atkinson, and Miles Papazian [Stephen Spinella], who is her number two. They added a new look to CTU and a hostile takeover, but we still have Chloe [Mary Lynn Rajskub] fighting the good fight for the good guys. The show really becomes Jack and Chloe, an outside/inside team."

All of the storylines ended up leading to what is arguably one of the best twists in the show's history, where Charles Logan is revealed as the wily conspirator behind the day's events, from Palmer's murder to the stolen Sentox gas that was supposed to be used against Russia to better the US's foreign oil interests in Central Asia. Surnow explains how Logan's twist came about: "The way our story goes is that we really hand off villains from arc to arc, and most seasons have two or three real villains. The point where we needed the next villain, it came to our attention that maybe the President was the villain. It was one of those 'Nina Myers — can this actually work?' moments. When we realized it could, we knew we could take this story to a whole other place."

Katz continues, "The season ended up being structured in a way that gave us places to evolve the

story, so instead of being stuck with a threat too long, we were able to not only change the story into a political story, but we were able to maneuver into it becoming Jack versus the President of the United States, and you can't get any bigger than that."

While the turn of events came organically, Gordon says the twist only held up because of the strength of the story that was attached to it. "Once we determined that Logan was going to be the villain in episode sixteen it gave shape to the rest of the season. Everything could hang on the spine of that antagonism, particularly when Jack was the only one who had the point of view that Logan was the bad guy. It really suggested that everything that came downstream from that was a variation on the theme."

In the thrilling final episodes, the writers were able to play with the audience's expectations as they moved toward the anticipated showdown between Logan and Jack. Robert Cochran got the pleasure of writing their tension-filled meeting in the abandoned machinery warehouse. While so much hinged on that moment, Cochran says it was easy because he knew he was writing for "...two great performers like Kiefer and Greg

Itzin. You know that if you can get anywhere near a good scene on paper, these guys are going to take it to the next level and really make it work. I enjoy writing that kind of scene because you know what the conflict is and you have two great performers."

Yet with Logan's unparalleled luck and ability to manipulate, the writers admit they toyed with the idea of Jack losing in the end. Coto confirms, "There was definitely some consideration at one point that Logan would actually get away with it. We thought that the audience might be satisfied enough with us taking out the two main villains, Henderson and Bierko, but the principal bad guy would get away. But Logan was such a prominent villain. He was such a forceful personality and an unpleasant character that as the season unfolded we began to feel that it would be such an unsatisfying experience if Logan didn't get some kind of comeuppance, so we adjusted our story to let him have his due. Plus, people really liked Martha and if Logan got away with it, where does that leave her? The answer is not in a very good place. At one point, we considered Logan getting away with it and Martha going to an asylum — a pretty dark ending. I think we came to our senses, but it's still a fairly dark ending. The President is arrested so it's not a happy time."

On some shows, resolving a major storyline like Logan's would be more than enough for an amazing finale, but the writers still had one more zinger to pull on audiences — the return of the vengeful Chinese. Gordon says, "We always knew the end would be this face-off between Logan and Jack, but people were always asking about the Chinese. They were our ace in the hole that we knew we had to play at some point, and it became a great way to end the year."

Cochran says their return to kidnap Jack when everything else had finally come back into balance was the perfect shock to write. "What was fun for me was that it was completely unexpected and yet it made sense for people that had been following the show. From the point of view of the Chinese, Jack had it coming. It came out of something that he did, so there was logic to it. It was shocking but not unreasonable, which is what you try to do when you do the cliffhanger thing."

And again, reinforcing the tragic hero that Jack Bauer has become, he has to sacrifice the things he holds most dear in service to his country. Surnow

offers, "On some level the season was Jack's long road back to Audrey to try and find a life again now that he is back in the world. Then when he finally gets it, of course it's taken away from him. He's indomitable and he's very self-sacrificing."

As a whole, the writers say they are most satisfied with how the season five stories threaded together on a variety of levels. Gordon assesses, "The great part of this show is that it's this continuing narrative that takes place over the course of twenty-four hours. I always view the year as a whole. The fact that you tell a story with a beginning, middle and an end, and where the beginning is as compelling as the middle and the end, is a great achievement. To tell one story with that many threads is great. I would say a not insignificant thing was that we brought on David Fury and Manny Coto. It was the first time we expanded the writing staff by that number of people and did it so successfully. Their learning curve was steep because they were jumping on a moving train. I had worked with both of them before and to get to work with them again was great. This show continues to be, up and down the hallway, one of the greatest places to work. People love being here and it's great to work with everybody. By and large I think the consensus, amongst fans as well, was that it didn't feel like season five had the mid-season lag. It just never really let up, so I'm really proud of that year."

Dead Man Talking: An Interview with Kiefer Sutherland

Over four seasons in his struggle to keep his country and its citizens safe, Jack Bauer has battled an astounding array of terrorists of every race and both genders, ruthless drug cartels, a murderous ex-girlfriend and even the country of China. For his selfless efforts, he's been rewarded in kind with countless beatings, the loss of his beloved wife, a broken relationship with his daughter, and a host of superiors all the way up to the White House that have contemplated snuffing him out.

At the end of season four, Jack made the decision to walk away from everything: career, family; in short, his life. Faking his death with the help of Tony Almeida, Michelle Dessler, Chloe O'Brian and former President David Palmer, Bauer was able to find an uneasy peace, shedding the burdens of his singular talents in the anonymity of 'death'. If that had been where Jack Bauer's story ended, then his walk along sun-dappled train tracks to nowhere would have been a bittersweet coda to the life of one remarkable man. But that's not the end in television, where a new season awaits only eight months away. For the fifth season of 24, the producers and Kiefer Sutherland had to bring the legend back from the dead like the fabled phoenix... just with guns.

While many shows have attempted the character resurrection, few have been able to credibly bring it off in a narrative that felt earned. In the case of 24, the writers were wise enough to keep the reason for Jack Bauer's return to his former life simple — retribution. By having assassins kill Palmer, Dessler and mortally wound Almeida, Bauer is provoked on the gut level to, again, willingly sacrifice his safety so that he is able to not only protect O'Brian, but also follow through on the conspiracy until the ultimate justice is served.

Chilling in its focus, while cleverly balancing some jaw-dropping revelations over the course of the day, season five maintained a momentum and singular vision that helped it ride a wave of critical and audience acclaim to an Emmy for Best Dramatic Series, along with Best Performance as a Lead Actor in a Dramatic Series for Kiefer Sutherland.

Breaking down why season five worked so well, Sutherland muses that the key to its success really comes down to the smaller beats. "It wasn't so much that this season was special, because there are things in every one of the years that I really liked and there are things that I really didn't. I think that the time format and everything else makes working on the show, from a writer's perspective, so restrictive. But I think the writers have done a fantastic job allowing me to have an emotional range. I think one of the things I've learned more on this show than at any other time in my career is that when you go from film to film you can make very broad choices from one project to another. This show has taught me about working with minutiae and making fifteen small changes over the course of one season to another.

"I also think that because we've been dong this for five years, every year has become a little easier," Sutherland continues. "I can't express to you how difficult it is for the writers. As constraining as the time format has been for the actors, it has been equally restrictive for the writers. Certainly from season two on, we learned that almost every eight episodes, whether it's conscious or not, the story takes a massive shift which breaks the season down into thirds. Even though there is absolutely no end trajectory that we are aiming at, there are conversations about where we're potentially aiming

at. There are conversations about the potentials of where the season can go and, even though they're simply conversations, every season I have noticed there will be traces of those conversations in all of those endings. So we're not working towards a void, but it certainly is open-ended."

As an executive producer on the series, along with his acting duties, Sutherland says he remains connected to the narrative process by continuing to engage the writers in an ongoing dialogue throughout the season, which makes them all accountable for maintaining the level of quality they collectively demand in the final product. "I think over time, certainly in the first year, almost all of the kind of passionate discussions between Joel Surnow or Bob Cochran or Howard Gordon or Evan Katz and myself really came out of the fear of not knowing where we were going and it being so different than any other experience I'd had. After five years I think we've got some faith in the way we've been figuring this out. Again, this whole experience has been a learning curve because I've certainly never done a real-time show; the producers have never written one before this; and none of the other actors have been a part of one. Literally, the first eight episodes of any season have taught us how to do the next eight and then,

again, the next eight. I think as soon as we all trusted that and accepted that, our lives got a lot easier and the shows got better."

Bringing back Jack Bauer as a loose cannon this year, with personal motivations compelling his actions rather than the tether of his government affiliations, meant a much freer canvas to explore. "The unique aspect for me this year, and the challenge for me this year, is that Jack doesn't work for CTU," Sutherland explains. "The fact that they were able to bring Jack back in a way that wasn't going to make him do the same stuff with CTU... Well, it was clear [from his actions] he wasn't working for CTU," he chuckles. "I think the writers have given him a lot of room to move. He was working from a very different perspective and he was not bound by the regulations of that job. Everything that he is doing this year is from an emotional response to a series of events. He was bound only by a clear sense of right and wrong and his determination to avenge the death of David Palmer. This is not about duty. This is not about a sense of responsibility. Those are very small changes; yet, how to try and inject those into this character and separate him, on a very small level, from last year or the year before, is an incredible challenge and something I've enjoyed immensely. I think when Jack Bauer gets to work from the perspective of something almost narrow, where he has one bone in his mouth, he tends to chew it until it falls apart," he laughs. "I responded to him as an actor in that capacity and I think audiences did as well."

While the show still remains focused on Jack Bauer every year, it has expanded monumentally from the first season. It now seems almost quaint to think back on the Bauers' search for their rebellious daughter against the backdrop of preventing the assassination of a Presidential candidate. Since then the stakes have ratcheted into the stratosphere, with world wars and nuclear holocausts being prevented on domestic soil. Critics and audiences have come to crave the addictive adrenaline rush that comes with the action sequences on the show now, but Sutherland is very quick to denounce the show's being pigeonholed as just action fare. "I think calling it an action show would be terribly unfair to the writers, who have written something so much more topical than that.

They have dealt with so many levels. It's also a real testament to Jon Cassar as to what they have been able to accomplish shooting-wise. You can't deny that the action in the show is really quite extraordinary. It's due to our crew and how well they work together. It's very hard to do on our schedule, but they have been able to make that work well. But I really believe it's a fusion. We started out as a real bare-to-the-bones thriller and it's morphed into an action thriller."

Sutherland also says that he's proud the writers have been able to remain resolute in their storytelling, not shying from the controversial issues of Muslim extremism or, in season five, depicting the fall from grace of the Commander-in-Chief of the United States. "This idea that we would have to placate an audience on any level because they can't 'get' something is absolutely wrong," the actor asserts passionately. "Our audiences are incredibly smart. We have to make the show the way we make it. I think Joel and Bob are right: if you work under the guise of what you think will win the audience, it's a mistake. You have to make what you think is right and hopefully, they will be there."

Citing a particular example, Sutherland says the controversial storyline involving President Logan helped invigorate the series and elevate it to another level. "I thought the writers did a fantastic job and that really energized the show. I think in many regards, I was doing things that were very similar to what Jack Bauer had done before, but, in that specific instance, there was this other killer storyline which was so fantastic and intriguing that it really balanced out the show."

Assessing the year as a whole, Sutherland says he is happy with where Jack started and where he ultimately landed, bumps and all. "This season, there wasn't one specific episode, for instance, that we make fun of or have been made fun of for, like [Kim] and the cougar," he smiles. "We didn't have that in season five. We didn't really have that in season four either, so the writers have done a fantastic job steering clear of that. But you always tend to think about things that could happen, like maybe wanting the Chinese to be involved a little earlier. A lot of my hopes for something to have been a little different weren't even seen in the show, but were just an option

of where we could have gone and where we didn't go. Each year we all work on that."

After five seasons, Kiefer Sutherland has more than one hundred and twenty hours of *24* under his belt and an Emmy for crafting a character that has become an icon around the globe. Yet, as always, Sutherland says it comes back down to just enjoying what he does. "I love playing the character and it's something I care an awful lot about. I'm committed to the show as long as I feel that we're moving forward and as long as the audience will allow me to do it."

DAY FIVE

7:00 am - 8:00 am

Director: Jon Cassar
Writer: Howard Gordon

Special Guest Stars: Reiko Aylesworth (Michelle Dessler), Dennis Haysbert (President David Palmer) Guest Cast: Connie Britton (Diane Huxley), Jude Ciccolella (Mike Novick), Jeff Kober (Haas)

> "I look like a wedding cake."
> First Lady Martha Logan

Timeframe

7:00 A.M. Jack Bauer is working in the Mohave under the alias 'Frank Flynn'.

7:02 A.M. In LA, David Palmer is assassinated by a sniper named Haas.

7:04 A.M. In the Western White House, Mike Novick and Walt Cummings prep President Charles Logan for a treaty signing with the Russian President. They learn of Palmer's murder.

7:07 A.M. Logan calls Bill Buchanan at CTU and demands they find the assassin.

7:08 A.M. Chloe O'Brian wakes up with CTU subordinate Spenser Wolff.

7:11 A.M. Jack has breakfast with his girlfriend, Diane Huxley, and her son, Derek.

7:13 A.M. Tony Almeida and Michelle Dessler learn of Palmer's death. She goes to CTU to help. Her car explodes and she dies. Tony is hurt in a second blast.

7:21 A.M. At CTU, Edgar calls Chloe about Tony and Michelle. Chloe is followed by Haas in a white van.

7:23 A.M. Chloe calls Jack about Tony and Michelle and asks for help. He gives her the location of an oil refinery and sets out to meet her.

7:25 A.M. Injured Tony is sent to CTU, as Audrey Raines arrives.

7:28 A.M. Cummings tells First Lady Martha Logan about Palmer's death. She becomes unbalanced.

7:37 A.M. Jack gets to the refinery and commandeers a chopper. Derek has followed Jack.

7:40 A.M. Logan talks to Martha, who says she spoke to Palmer the day before and thinks she might be somehow involved. Logan doesn't believe her.

7:42 A.M. Logan tells Cummings that Martha is delusional.

7:52 A.M. Chloe arrives at the refinery and meets Jack.

7:53 A.M. Haas and his men arrive. Jack takes the men out.

7:54 A.M. Haas finds Chloe and Derek. Jack shoots him in the leg.

7:55 A.M. Before he kills him, Jack gets Haas to admit he was hired to kill Palmer.

Key Events

David Palmer is assassinated.

Tony and Michelle are targeted.

Martha Logan has a meltdown.

As usual, co-executive producer Jon Cassar kicked off the new season by directing the first two episodes. The seminal moment of the first hour was former President David Palmer's shocking assassination. It was filmed in an empty penthouse in the upscale Wilshire Corridor, which is a very rare location for film production due to the expensive housing. Cassar framed the terrible scene using inspiration from events in actual history. "I didn't want to see it coming," the director explains. "I wanted it to be as much a shock to the audience as it was to [Palmer]. I played on the collective memories of assassinations we've all grown up with. It's that image of Martin Luther King and that guy standing on the balcony pointing, so that alludes to

the balcony in the window. Then there is the image of DB [Woodside] cradling Dennis in his arms, just like the guy did with Robert Kennedy in the kitchen. And because he wasn't a President anymore, it couldn't be as public as the JFK assassination, but I still wanted those images to be in your head. It felt like something maybe you had seen before and didn't know why. I think it worked out well."

The opening hour also showed a new side to Chloe, which immediately energized actress Mary Lynn Rajskub. "I was really excited at the beginning of the year because I was in bed with somebody and then I got to have my hair down and run and get chased and knock some people over. I got to shoot somebody! We went downtown one day and there were people everywhere and traffic everywhere. I couldn't tell which were ours and which were our extras. There were real cabs and within three minutes they had the whole street locked down because they are used to doing these elaborate shoots. It was pretty amazing to be a part of that. I could get used to it. I like it!"

Research Files

The Western White House: Instead of hosting Russian President Suvarov in Washington DC, President Logan welcomes him to his residence in Hidden Valley, California (near Westlake Village). Dubbed the Western White House, the term actually applies to any residence the President works from that is outside of the White House. The first President to create a Western White House was Franklin Delano Roosevelt, who spent time at the Royal Hawaiian Hotel in Honolulu, Hawaii during World War II. Other important alternative presidential addresses included Camp David, Maryland (named after Eisenhower's grandson); Reagan's Rancho del Cielo in California; Nixon's La Casa Pacifica home in California; Ford's The Lodge in Vail, Colorado; and George W. Bush's Prairie Chapel Ranch in Crawford, Texas. Once a President names an outside residence, federal money can then be used to create a work environment that allows the Executive-in-Chief to be properly connected to the necessary government agencies.

Additional Intel

During the opening scene, the foreman calls out the names of rig workers, which happen to be the names of real *24* crew members: Jim Nichols, Sterling Rush (set prop master), Patrick Priest (key set PA), Phil Stone (construction coordinator) and Greg Nelson.

8:00 am - 9:00 am

Director: Jon Cassar
Writer: Evan Katz

Guest Cast: John Allen Nelson (Walt Cummings), Connie Britton (Diane Huxley), Jude Ciccolella (Mike Novick), DB Woodside (Wayne Palmer), Kathleen Gati (Anya Suvarov)

(To Derek) "Let's get something straight, kid. The only reason you're still conscious is because I don't want to carry you." Jack Bauer

Timeframe

8:03 A.M. Jack gets Chloe to access Palmer's residence.
8:04 A.M. Edgar confirms video from Palmer's apartment features Jack. Buchanan puts together the conspiracy.
8:05 A.M. Buchanan issues a warrant for Jack.
8:06 A.M. Audrey tells Logan that Bauer is the suspect.
8:15 A.M. In the assassin's van, Chloe uses her CTU ID to get into the building.
8:16 A.M. Chloe taps into the agents' transponder signals using the assassin's earwigs and Jack enters the building.
8:19 A.M. Jack sees Palmer's body and is upset.
8:20 A.M. Chloe explains to Derek who Jack really is.
8:21 A.M. Jack is found by Wayne Palmer. Jack says he was framed for David's murder and he needs Wayne's help.
8:25 A.M. Jack and Wayne find the encrypted first chapter to David's memoir.
8:26 A.M. Edgar discovers that Chloe is tapped into CTU.
8:27 A.M. Edgar alerts Buchanan to Chloe's location.
8:33 A.M. Wayne finds "Chevensky at 16 Transport Way" in the memoir. Jack tracks it to Ontario Airport and leaves Wayne to follow the trail.
8:35 A.M. Chloe loses her connection and Jack barely makes it out.
8:36 A.M. Chloe is surrounded by agents.
8:42 A.M. Meanwhile, Jack and Derek steal a car and call Diane.
8:43 A.M. Chloe tells Buchanan that Jack has been framed.
8:45 A.M. Logan tells Martha that Jack killed Palmer and plays back the call David made to her, which she says is false.
8:48 A.M. CTU confirms to Logan that Russian President Suvarov is a target.
8:56 A.M. Jack arrives at Ontario Airport. Suvarov arrives safely.
8:57 A.M. Derek sees strange men and runs to warn Jack.
8:58 A.M. Jack confronts Chevensky. A bomb explodes. Chevensky swallows poison.
8:59 A.M. Hostages are taken at the airport. Chloe is in handcuffs at CTU. Cummings secretly conspires with the terrorists.

Key Events

Jack sees Palmer's body.

Chloe gets arrested.

Cummings is revealed as the traitor.

The gorgeous, full scale Western White House set for season five was devised by production designer Joseph Hodges. "The new retreat took up the whole stage," Hodges details. "It started bigger, but during the build we ran out of time and money so it got smaller in terms of the materials we used. People say it's just television and it's not a feature, but to me it's more important to have great finishes on a television set because we are there the whole year, if not five years. The producers said this was only going to be in seven or eight episodes, but it lasted the entire season. When I did the original retreat for Palmer, I built it with courtyards so it had daylight and an outside feel, but the courtyard was too small to hold scenes in. For the new retreat, I built a huge courtyard

with a lap pool." Laughing, he adds: "You should never put water in a set, but I thought, 'Why not?' With such a big exterior space I figured if I put water along the front, the reflection off it would be great!"

Set decorator Cloudia Rebar did the interiors based on Hodges' theme of mid-century décor. "On my first day on season five, I found out what we were doing and realized that in five weeks the set had to be built and dressed, and the furniture would all have to be brand new pieces fabricated from scratch by the manufacturers. I realized I had about two hours to find everything and get the fabrics and start production because manufacturers usually want three months minimum. It was intense! Another challenge was the mid-century case goods because they are so hard to find and they are ridiculously expensive. Something that looks like it would be twenty-nine dollars is like 4,000 dollars! But the artwork was obtained from Joseph Hodges' father. They are originals and they lend themselves beautifully to the space. He would have done them about the time the President would have been a younger man and purchased them."

Research Files

LA/Ontario International Airport: Formerly known as Ontario Airport, this is the second largest airport in the southern California region and it's located in San Bernardino County. In 1923, the airport was actually built by one of the first flying clubs in southern California, known as The Friends of Ontario Airport. The expanded airport now hosts international flights and boasts two runways and three terminals. The airport hosts thirteen major carriers including American, US Air, Aeroméxico and Southwest. The airport also serves as a major hub for UPS and FedEx, and is the primary alternate landing designation for LAX Airport when bad weather or congestion keeps flights from landing at that location. On any given day, more than 350 flights take off and land from this location, as it is becoming a more popular alternative airport for travelers looking to bypass high traffic delays.

Additional Intel

Cloudia Rebar reveals that all of the lush plants in the retreat were high-end, specimen silk plants. Real plants are impossible to keep looking the same over ten months and would ruin continuity.

9:00 am - 10:00 am

Director: Brad Turner
Writer: Manny Coto

Guest Cast: Nick Jameson (Yuri Suvarov), Glenn Morshower (Agent Aaron Pierce), John Allen Nelson (Walt Cummings), Brady Corbet (Derek Huxley), Connie Britton (Diane Huxley)

"Understand this, Bill. I don't work for you. I'm staying inside. You want my intel, fine. But I'm doing this my way." Jack Bauer

Timeframe   Key Events

9:02 A.M. A gunman shoots a hostage.
9:04 A.M. The leader, Beresch, threatens to blow up the hostages.
9:05 A.M. Jack enters the air ducts.
9:06 A.M. The dead assassin at the refinery is found, exonerating Jack.
9:07 A.M. Jack sends images of the gunmen to Buchanan.
9:10 A.M. Buchanan reinstates Chloe. Edgar IDs Beresch.
9:12 A.M. Beresch demands the treaty summit be called off.
9:13 A.M. Logan is livid and refuses.
9:15 A.M. By phone, Diane reveals to Jack that Derek is inside the terminal.
9:23 A.M. Beresch shoots a hostage.
9:25 A.M. Beresch grabs Derek and gives a fifteen-minute ultimatum.
9:31 A.M. Martha believes the situation stems from Palmer's phone call to her. She asks her aide, Evelyn, to cover for her.
9:32 A.M. In a panic over Derek, Jack calls Chloe for help in finding a wireless detonation frequency for the vest bombs.
9:33 A.M. Chloe gets Spenser to help her reconfigure Jack's phone to emit an alternate signal. Edgar observes their unauthorized actions.
9:35 A.M. Martha sneaks up on a communications tech and demands his security card or she will scream.
9:44 A.M. Chloe tells Jack how to set the bomb off.
9:45 A.M. Jack detonates the wireless vest bomb.
9:46 A.M. Buchanan briefs Logan and explains Jack's involvement. Logan is angry.
9:52 A.M. Martha finds the transcript of her call with Palmer.
9:54 A.M. Agent Aaron Pierce finds Martha.
9:55 A.M. Cummings calls his conspirators about Jack. Pierce explains Martha's whereabouts and Cummings panics.
9:57 A.M. Jack's phone signal is blasted.
9:58 A.M. Over the loud speaker, Beresch demands Jack surrender or Derek dies. Jack reveals himself and is taken.

President Logan is livid at the terrorists.

Derek is about to be shot.

Jack surrenders to the terrorists.

Every season of *24* has a visual look that is created through the collaboration of the episode director, production designer Joseph Hodges and director of photography, Rodney Charters. In particular, the Ontario Airport hijacking episodes heavily influenced the look of the year. While the bulk was shot on location, Hodges reveals they rigged quite a bit to get the gritty feel of an actual terrorist event. "We put it together rather cleverly to match. I'm sure a lot of people watching the episode assume you can get into the airport ceiling, but most people watching don't have a clue that the hole doesn't really exist or Kiefer isn't really above the ceiling in an airport. When I do my job really well, it's invisible."

As to the unique lighting for the show, Charters explains, "We try to use existing, practical lighting that is the kind of light you would find in industrial spaces. It's often got a green spike to it because of the gases used in the lights, and we augment our lighting to match the tone. We keep it as grubby as we can and it makes for a very unhappy LA," he smiles. "For this season, I think the tone was set by the airport. It was very spare. It was a big building in a terminal that was no longer used, so the architecture was somewhat dated. We just wanted it to feel it could be real and I think we achieved that. I believe it was the kind of event you could have witnessed if you unhappily might have been a part of it, so the audience can share the paranoia and the fear. We see this information on television, with terrorist attacks, and they are often photographed by miniature cameras that people have in cell phones now. People know what these situations look like now, so we can't glamorize it. Once we set that tone we strive to keep it that way and stay out of the way of the story."

Research Files

Hostage Crisis: When the Russian terrorists seize Ontario Airport, they hold forty random hostages in the terminal against their will. The situation becomes an official hostage crisis when the terrorists barricade themselves inside the terminal and threaten the outside authorities that they will kill the innocent inside unless their demands are met. Every year there are many dramatic hostage crisis situations that happen throughout the world. Statistically, most hostage situations are on the small scale, involving mentally imbalanced or violent offenders. But there are some that have gathered global attention and even changed the course of history. Some standoffs lasted for mere hours, like the Munich Olympian massacre during the 1972 Olympics, where seven Israeli athletes and a German police officer were killed, or they can last for days, like the extreme 444 days of the Iran hostage crisis in the early eighties. Depending on the ultimate intentions of the hostage takers and the effectiveness of hostage negotiators, the situations end up ending about equal in terms of lives being saved and lives being taken.

Additional Intel

At the start of season five, writer/co-executive producer Manny Coto joined *24* and this was his first episode (co-written with Bob Cochran). The year before, Coto executive produced the last season of *Star Trek: Enterprise*.

10:00 am - 11:00 am

Director: Brad Turner
Writers: Joel Surnow & Michael Loceff

Guest Cast: Nick Jameson (Yuri Suvarov), John Allen Nelson (Walt Cummings), Jonah Lotan (Spenser Wolff), Brady Corbet (Derek Huxley), Sean Astin (Lynn McGill)

"Your President is a weak man. He'll back down once more blood is spilled." Anton Beresch

Timeframe	Key Events

10:01 A.M. Beresch confronts Jack about CTU's plan.

10:04 A.M. Beresch shoots another hostage. Logan wants to cave but Cummings advises otherwise.

10:06 A.M. Martha decides to hide the transcript in her bra.

10:08 A.M. Angered, Beresch tells Jack he will kill Derek next.

10:09 A.M. At CTU, Lynn McGill takes over command.

10:11 A.M. Forced, Jack calls Curtis with a "flank two" position for the terrorists.

10:17 A.M. Curtis needs fifteen minutes to reorganize. McGill demands approval before authorizing.

10:21 A.M. Suvarov arrives and Logan tells him of the situation.

10:22 A.M. Cummings threatens Evelyn and she explains the transcript and where Martha has hidden it.

10:29 A.M. Logan addresses the press about the terrorists and reaffirms his strong position.

10:32 A.M. McGill is suspicious of Jack's new location call and demands to read the transcripts.

10:34 A.M. A gunman finds Chevensky and a hidden key card. Jack sees Beresch pass the card to a "hostage" in a yellow tie.

10:39 A.M. Curtis calls Jack. Beresch makes Jack confirm the wrong flank position.

10:40 A.M. McGill calls off the attack, as he's cracked the meaning of Jack's "flank two" code. Curtis aborts.

10:43 A.M. The treaty is signed by Logan and Suvarov. CTU attacks in the right position, killing the gunmen.

10:44 A.M. Beresch detonates one of his men's vests and dies. The hostages are freed.

10:45 A.M. Logan announces his authorized rescue operation was a success.

10:51 A.M. Jack notices "yellow tie" is missing.

10:52 A.M. Martha demands to talk to Logan, who refuses.

10:54 A.M. McGill wants Jack brought to CTU for questioning.

10:57 A.M. "Yellow tie" enters a sublevel hangar and with the key card, several radioactive canisters are released.

10:58 A.M. Cummings chloroforms Martha and takes the transcript.

Logan and Suvarov sign the treaty.

"Yellow tie" unlocks the canisters.

Cummings attacks Martha.

The Ontario Airport storyline ended up being director Brad Turner's first big set piece of the season. "The biggest challenge of Ontario was, as with any hostage situation, to make it interesting visually because you are stuck in one place. There was a bit of repetition to the scenes we shot there because there was an ongoing threat of a hostage being taken. Every move in that arena had to be told a little differently, and so it was interesting when [Beresch] started selecting hostages. It's all about choreographing and selecting the next person that is different looking; you need to block them all differently. Also, working in a big arena, you have to decide how you are going to shoot and in what order. I'm a big fan of shooting everything in order as

much as possible, especially on this show. My choice is to always shoot the most important parts, like the area where people are being assassinated, so I can get the emotional thing going. Overall, I thought the whole thing turned out pretty good. It had a really nice pace."

As mentioned by Joseph Hodges, Turner says what audiences don't know about the production is what the team considers to be the most successful aspect. "The thing I am really proud of is that Kiefer up in the rafters was shot completely in studio. The camera was on a lift and I shot it through a piece of set dressing so it looked like Jack was looking through the roof. I shot all the point-of-view stuff first, the stuff he was watching, then we built the set on stage and I talked Kiefer through what he was 'seeing', including the stuff when he gets in the wall and is looking out of the side. We created that solely from standing on location and looking up and seeing the design of the ceiling and the wall. When in fact there was no room to do anything; all of it was created from a cheated point of view, so production wise I was most proud of that."

Research Files

Chloroform: Walt Cummings subdues Martha Logan by applying a cloth with chloroform to her face. Also known as trichloromethane and methyl trichloride, chloroform has long been used as an anesthetic. The chemical substance was first produced in 1831 in both the US and France, but it wasn't until 1847 that Edinburgh obstetrician James Young Simpson used chloroform as a general anesthesia during a standard childbirth. The success of that usage made the use of chloroform spread throughout Europe and eventually, it replaced ether use in the United States. Unfortunately, it wasn't long before the side effects of chloroform became apparent when many patients came down with fatal cardiac arrhythmia as a direct result of its use. Therefore, it has been all but phased out except for in some developing nations that still rely on it as a cost-effective anesthetic. Today, chloroform is primarily used in the production of Freon for refrigeration and as a solvent.

Additional Intel

This episode was the 100th episode of *24*. To celebrate, Fox threw a party for the cast and crew at the Cabana Club in Hollywood on January 7, 2006. The producers created a highlight reel of all 100 episodes for the event that is included on the season five DVD.

11:00 am - 12:00 pm

Director: Jon Cassar
Writers: Joel Surnow & Michael Loceff

Guest Cast: Jude Ciccolella (Mike Novick), Mark A. Sheppard (Ivan Erwich), John Allen Nelson (Walt Cummings), Connie Britton (Diane Huxley), Sean Astin (Lynn McGill)

"When we find the nerve gas and the alert level goes down, we can sit down with some chamomile tea and I will tell you all my secrets." Chloe O'Brian

Timeframe — Key Events

11:00 A.M. In a fake SWAT truck, "yellow tie" and his men exit the airport.

11:03 A.M. Evelyn finds Martha passed out.

11:04 A.M. Curtis finds security footage with "yellow tie" fleeing.

11:06 A.M. Curtis finds the empty hanger and dead rats. He calls biohazard.

11:07 A.M. "Yellow tie" and his men transfer the canisters to a new truck and reveal the plan to bomb Moscow.

11:08 A.M. A groggy Martha tells Logan that she was knocked out. He doesn't believe her.

11:10 A.M. Cummings advises Logan to have Martha committed and he agrees.

11:18 A.M. Novick alerts Logan that terrorists escaped the airport.

11:21 A.M. Spenser receives a secret page from Cummings asking about Bauer.

11:22 A.M. At CTU, McGill has Audrey question Diane.

11:28 A.M. CTU comes to a standstill as Jack returns. McGill clears Jack of Palmer's murder and briefs him on the nerve gas.

11:33 A.M. Audrey reunites with Jack. He explains his disappearance and she admits she forgave him for Paul's death.

11:34 A.M. Cummings has Evelyn pack Martha's belongings.

11:35 A.M. Chloe discovers Spenser is logged in with a level five security clearance. Edgar confirms Spenser is level three, so she alerts Buchanan.

11:37 A.M. Spenser lets "yellow tie"'s accomplice, Hank, into CTU.

11:46 A.M. Spenser is locked out of his computer and brought before Buchanan and Chloe.

11:47 A.M. Logan and Cummings find Martha has fled.

11:53 A.M. Medical calls to say Tony is conscious and requesting Jack.

11:56 A.M. In Medical, Hank attacks Jack. Hank receives a pair of scissors to the throat.

11:58 A.M. Jack confronts Spenser, who admits he was under the orders of Cummings to monitor CTU.

11:59 A.M. Jack goes after Cummings for Palmer's death.

Audrey and Jack meet again.

Jack scissors the bad guy.

Jack is going after Cummings.

Actress Kim Raver returns to *24* as Jack's love and Department of Defense liaison at CTU. Unlike the previous year, Audrey becomes a big part of the CTU operation for the season, a change that Raver loved. "I thought it was great to put her in CTU because she is out of her element. CTU is not her arena, but what was great is Audrey getting to do her job the best that she can in that environment, while getting to know Edgar and Chloe. I loved the way she went from being so by the book to doing what she thinks is best for the country. What she does and what she's passionate about is the love of her country. How she does it changed in season five and to me that's really interesting because it's more like Jack. She's willing to go behind the backs of

the people that were running CTU to do the things necessary to accomplish what she believes is best for the country."

Speaking of Jack, the former lovers reunite this day with more mutual understanding. But striking the right romantic balance was important, Raver says. "Kiefer and I had constant discussions about the relationship. I think the pitfall would be for it to be just about the relationship. That would be very melodramatic and the world keeps turning in the end, so who really cares about the relationship? I think the key and the fine line, what really makes *24* for me, is that there is an explosion and a car chase, a car crash and chasing after nuclear weapons, and that works for me because there is an emotional connection to other people. It's not just about that connection, but when you have that, the stakes of saving the day are so much higher. That's why the Logan story worked, because you start to understand and care who these people are, so when a gun is put to someone's head, there is a real visceral reaction. The action is the active part of the show and the relationships, hopefully, heighten that part."

Research Files

Nerve Gas: The Russians get in their possession several canisters of the fictional nerve gas, Sentox VX-1, which they plan to unleash on heavily populated areas in the United States. A nerve gas is a vaporous (or liquid at room temperature) chemical that disrupts the way nerves transfer messages to the organs. Because of their incredibly lethal effects, nerve agents and gases are considered weapons of mass destruction by governments around the world and have been outlawed, according to the Chemical Weapons Convention ratified by the United Nations in 1997. Exposure to a nerve agent is particularly toxic with symptoms including convulsions, loss of bladder and bowel control, salivation and, eventually, death by asphyxiation. There are two main classes of nerve agents: the G and V series. The G-Series is named 'G' after the German scientists that first synthesized them during World War II and the V-series (which stands for venomous) was invented in the United Kingdom.

Additional Intel

Twenty Sentox gas canisters were designed and fabricated by property master Randy Gunter. The original design featured a mechanized centerpiece that rose from the canister, but the idea was scrapped due to the storyline.

Jack Bauer

Experience:

Department of Defense, Washington DC – Special Assistant to the Secretary of Defense
CTU – Director of Field Operations, Los Angeles Domestic Unit
CTU – Special Agent in Charge, Los Angeles Domestic Unit
Los Angeles PD – Special Weapons and Tactics

Expertise:

Basic SWAT School – LASD
University of California (Berkeley) – Master of Science, Criminology and Law
University of California (Los Angeles) – Bachelor of Arts, English Literature
Special Forces Operations Training Course

Military:

US Army – Combat Applications Group, Delta Force
Counter Terrorist Group

Personal:

Spouse – Teri Bauer (deceased)
Daughter – Kimberly Bauer

12:00 pm - 1:00 pm

Director: Jon Cassar
Writer: David Fury

Guest Cast: Mark A. Sheppard (Ivan Erwich), John Allen Nelson (Walt Cummings), Sandrine Holt (Evelyn), Jude Ciccolella (Mike Novick), Glenn Morshower (Agent Aaron Pierce)

(To Audrey) "I never stopped loving you. Not for one second." Jack Bauer

Timeframe	Key Events

12:04 P.M. "Yellow tie" and his accomplice Schaeffer send the gas to Moscow.

12:05 P.M. Logan is upset about Martha. Novick gets a text message from Jack. Cummings is very nervous.

12:06 P.M. Novick calls Jack, who arranges a meeting.

12:07 P.M. Jack sends Diane and Derek home. Jack admits he still loves Audrey.

12:09 P.M. Cummings is ordered to kill Jack at the retreat.

12:14 P.M. Agent Pierce finds Martha in the stables. She begs for his help.

12:17 P.M. Schaeffer secretly attaches a device to the canisters and locks it.

12:20 P.M. Agent Pierce tells Logan he found Martha.

12:21 P.M. Cummings tells Logan that Jack is on his way. He confesses to leaking information to the terrorists, but says the canisters are rigged to detonate before they get to Russia. It's a plan to help America increase its presence in Central Asia and obtain oil.

12:23 P.M. Logan demands the scheme is stopped. Cummings says it is too late and if he doesn't comply, Logan will be implicated too.

12:29 P.M. Novick meets with Jack but the Secret Service arrive and arrest Jack.

12:31 P.M. Cummings plans to frame Jack. Logan authorizes Cummings to take CTU off the case.

12:34 P.M. Buchanan persuades McGill to disregard the order.

12:36 P.M. Jack reveals the truth about Palmer to Agent Pierce.

12:44 P.M. Jack is shocked Logan knows Cummings' plans. Jack threatens Cummings for the nerve gas location.

12:47 P.M. Logan explains to Jack he was coerced. He reinstates CTU and has Jack promise to disappear again after the threat is over.

12:57 P.M. CTU finds the ship. Schaeffer is dead and the canisters have disappeared.

12:59 P.M. Cummings' cell rings; it's "yellow tie" (aka Ivan Erwich). He says Schaeffer confessed and now the country will pay.

Martha asks Agent Pierce for help.

Jack is surrounded.

Cummings gets a Bauer-style interrogation.

The confrontation between Bill Buchanan and Lynn McGill in this episode showcases the disparity in experience between the two men. Executive producer Howard Gordon explains that McGill being so overwhelmed was the lynchpin of the character. "Lynn was a very fun archetype. It was really a way to have Bill Buchanan experience something. Buchanan is this rock-solid, down-the-middle character, and to have him answerable to a "superior" who is younger than him and less experienced, but out-ranks him, was a very fun thing. There is a movie like it, with Dennis Quaid and Topher Grace called *In Good Company*, so we did our own version of that."

Co-creator Joel Surnow adds, "Lynn comes in and you make

him a jerk, and then he saves the day and he's not such a jerk. I think that's a classic *24* move. Just as you are learning to hate a guy, he does something to make you like him. The first guy we did that with on the show was George Mason."

Actor James Morrison remembers about the scene, "I have a pretty important speech to Lynn, who is young and inexperienced and thrust into a situation that he's not quite ready for without knowing why, because again, he's only told half of the information. I say to him, these are the things you have to do to be successful at what you've been asked to do here. One of the things is learning how to make decisions faster." Chuckling, Morrison adds, "Nobody can think at the speed that Jack and Buchanan think at! We are sort of super-human in that way and I think we have to be to stay ahead of the audience."

As to McGill's overall arc, actor Sean Astin says gleefully that all he really wanted was a good death. "In terms of expectations, I knew I would be dying soon — you could feel it coming. I hoped in the back of my mind, maybe they would make me the villain, which would be kind of cool, but then I thought that's not really Lynn, so hopefully they don't just give me a fool's end. They didn't, so I was grateful."

Research Files

Moscow: Erwin and Schaeffer intend to ship the Sentox gas to Moscow for its eventual use against Russia. Moscow became the capital of Russia in 1480 at the hands of Ivan III. Named after the Moskva River that flows beside the city, Moscow has a population of more than ten million and houses seven percent of the country's total population. The city has been the stage for many uprisings in its long, contentious history, with the most notable being the Russian Revolution of 1917 which ushered in Communism. In 1991, Communism fell and Moscow became the national seat of power for the Russian Federation. The Kremlin houses the President of Russia, while the 417 square miles of the city is governed by one mayor. The city hosted the 1980 Summer Olympic games. Today, Moscow is known both as the cultural and business center of the country.

Additional Intel

This episode marked the first episode writing credit for co-executive producer David Fury (*Lost*, *Buffy the Vampire Slayer* and *Angel*). He reveals that Howard Gordon gave a shout out to former *Buffy* writer Jane Espenson in episode ten by naming a character after her.

1:00 pm - 2:00 pm

Director: Brad Turner
Writer: Manny Coto

Guest Cast: John Allen Nelson (Walt Cummings), Mark A. Sheppard (Ivan Erwich), Sean Astin (Lynn McGill), Jude Ciccolella (Mike Novick), Glenn Morshower (Agent Aaron Pierce)

"When I am done with you, you are going to wish you felt this good again." Jack Bauer

Timeframe	Key Events

1:00 P.M. Cummings says he was recruited by a man named Nathanson to secure oil interests. The terrorists have gone rogue.

1:04 P.M. Jack offers to disappear, but Logan reinstates him to find the nerve gas.

1:06 P.M. McGill's junkie sister, Jenny, calls asking for money. She threatens to hurt herself and so he agrees to meet her.

1:08 P.M. Erwich calls Jacob Rossler to install new detonation codes on the canisters.

1:09 P.M. Chloe manages to track Erwich and Rossler to downtown LA.

1:10 P.M. Jack, by helicopter, and Curtis, by ground, are dispatched.

1:11 P.M. Chloe enlists Spenser's help to hack into Rossler's office's security system. Jack asks Audrey to have Kim brought to CTU.

1:19 P.M. Novick proposes covering up Cummings' treason but Martha disagrees. Logan asks her to write a statement for him.

1:21 P.M. Erwich forces a mechanic to help him cut the canisters.

1:33 P.M. Spenser is able to disable the security cameras so Jack and Curtis can get inside.

1:35 P.M. Jack shoots Rossler in the leg and finds a young woman being held captive in the penthouse.

1:37 P.M. Jack and Curtis work Rossler over, but he demands full immunity and the girl.

1:39 P.M. McGill grants his requests. Rossler wants it signed by the Attorney General.

1:44 P.M. McGill meets his sister and is jumped and mugged by her boyfriend. They escape.

1:46 P.M. Rossler explains he is waiting for a call from Erwich to reprogram the canisters.

1:55 P.M. Logan and Martha find Cummings has hanged himself.

1:58 P.M. With the canisters all cut, Erwich kills the mechanic and calls Rossler. He texts the codes over for Rossler to do his work.

1:59 P.M. The young girl shoots Rossler and the link to Erwich is gone.

McGill gets jumped.

Cummings is found dead.

Rossler's captive gets revenge.

After spending four seasons as a periphery character, Agent Aaron Pierce steps out of the Secret Service shadows this year. Surprisingly, Pierce's direct connection to the story is Martha Logan. Cast aside by her husband, Martha turns to Pierce to believe her story about Palmer's death. Co-executive producer David Fury explains, "Aaron had worked for David Palmer and we established very early on that Martha and David were very close. When Aaron was brought back into the story, we thought it would be a nice thing if Aaron had a little thing for Martha. It was an outlet and a little light in the tunnel. I may have been one of the first to hint at it in episode six, but it was something we just decided to expand on and to keep going with."

After Pierce protects Martha during the motorcade attack, audiences quickly picked up on the duos subtle chemistry. Story editor Matt Michnovetz and script coordinator Nicole Ranadive explain that their story was tricky to write. "We were really concerned about being able to do it right, so he didn't look like a back door man, so to speak," Michnovetz says. Ranadive adds, "They had a great chemistry though. I think Jean and Greg had fantastic chemistry, but then Jean and Glenn did some great work too because it was really subtle. You bought it and believed that they couldn't be together but they wanted to be."

As the season rolled on, Fury explains, "Aaron became a bigger player in the conspiracy to bring down the President, so it gave some stakes to Martha. Again, we try to find what the history is of these characters and the shared histories and if they can have a history together. Aaron resonated with the fans quite a bit, long before we gave him anything to do. They like constants. Here is a guy who has Jack Bauer's sense of honor and duty. Even though he is very quietly on the sidelines, people really responded to that. To be able to give him an emotional life was an extra bonus to be able to throw into year five."

Research Files

Russian Slave Trade: Jacob Rossler holds a young Russian woman in his penthouse as a sex slave, until she turns the tables on her tormentor and shoots him dead. Her situation reflects the reality of a multi-billion dollar industry around the world that is trafficking a large number of Russian and Eastern European women to the highest bidder. The collapse of Communism in the former Soviet Union opened up a new industry where women, especially from the countries of Ukraine, Belarus, Latvia and Russia, are shipped around the world for prostitution. According to the United Nations, an estimated one million women each year are exploited for sex industries, with Russian women in particular, located in more than fifty countries. The young women are almost always lured by underground traffickers through ads promising educational opportunities, or jobs available overseas.

Additional Intel

A big fan of the series, US Senator John McCain was invited by the producers to appear in this episode in a non-speaking, uncredited cameo. He appears in CTU as an employee who hands Audrey Raines a folder.

2:00 pm - 3:00 pm

Director: Brad Turner
Writers: Robert Cochran & Evan Katz

Guest Cast: Mark A. Sheppard (Ivan Erwich), Robert Maffia (Andrei), Sandrine Holt (Evelyn), Jude Ciccolella (Mike Novick), Sean Astin (Lynn McGill)

(To Charles) "…It's your job to tell the truth, even when it's ugly. And if you don't, I will." Martha Logan

Timeframe	Key Events

2:00 P.M. A shaken McGill returns and is briefed on Rossler's death. Erwich calls.

2:01 P.M. Jack answers indistinctly and Erwich provides a meeting location.

2:02 P.M. Jack plans to pose as Rossler.

2:03 P.M. Curtis gives Jack a chip that also has a listening device.

2:05 P.M. Novick and Logan discuss covering up Cummings' suicide.

2:09 P.M. A van arrives at the rendezvous point and two men approach Jack for the chip.

2:11 P.M. One of the men punches Jack and puts him in the van.

2:12 P.M. Audrey wants to stop the plan, but McGill and Buchanan think it's the only way to find the canisters.

2:18 P.M. Martha is upset at the press statement calling Cummings a hero. She confronts her husband.

2:20 P.M. Inside the van, Jack realizes one of the canisters is present. They drive to a shopping mall.

2:22 P.M. CTU prepares to intercept the canister before they enter the mall. Jack is forced to follow the terrorists.

2:23 P.M. McGill decides to let the canister be detonated rather than lose the others. Buchanan calls the President.

2:30 P.M. Inside the mall, the terrorists kill a guard and open air ducts.

2:31 P.M. Jack listens as CTU tells Logan the situation.

2:33 P.M. Logan agrees to let the canister be used for the greater good of recovering the other nineteen.

2:34 P.M. Breaking orders, Jack provides the wrong activation code.

2:36 P.M. Erwich is called and instructed to manually arm the canisters.

2:44 P.M. Jack fights and manages to stop the full release of the canister.

2:48 P.M. Chloe tracks the chip held by the fleeing terrorist.

2:58 P.M. CTU surrounds the mechanic shop where Erwich has the canisters.

2:59 P.M. Erwich escapes in a pick up with the canisters as CTU raids.

The mall is attacked!

Martha has to lie to Cummings' wife.

Erwich gets away.

The episode where Jack tries to thwart the terrorists from releasing the Sentox gas into a mall was another large-scale location shoot that fell to director Brad Turner to coordinate and shoot. Kiefer Sutherland and the crew went on location and used real patrons as extras for the intense food court scene. "We came in at five in the morning and we had to be finished in the mall eating area by lunchtime," Turner explains about the production day. "This sequence was much more complicated than the airport, which was completely controlled. This was in a working shopping mall, so we had to shoot totally out of sequence. Obviously, we needed the big look of a mall, and it was one we have visited before because it is very film friendly. So the

shooting was done around the needs of the mall. For the most part, we were able to shoot during business hours, such as when they first run into the mall and when Kiefer is brought in, and then when the outbreak happens and he comes out into the food court. We had to begin with the very emotional stuff, so when the gas escapes in the mall — that scene was done first. We ended up going back to the beginning of the sequence when the mall was open for business, because it was just our guys walking into the mall as repairmen. After that we designed a security control room where they install the gas into the ventilation system. We built that set in the mall in an empty room. The whole ventilation system was our set piece that we stuck in an unused room. Those are the things you have to do. We did all the mall scenes, plus the engineering room, in one day. It was a really long day, like sixteen-hours long." Smiling, Turner adds, "Days like that put me on my game harder and I like to take on the challenge."

Research Files

Treason: Mike Novick and President Logan decide to cover up Walt Cummings' death as a suicide rather than expose his treason. Officially defined as a crime of loyalty against one's nation, treason has been an issue for governments since the beginning of recorded history. In the United States, treason is the only crime specifically defined in the United States Constitution. Therefore, the United States Code requires that any US citizen proved to have committed treason serves no less than five years in prison, pays a fine of no less than ten thousand dollars and can never hold public office in the United States. It is actually a rarely tried crime with less than forty people being prosecuted for treason and even fewer being convicted. Famous treason cases include Aaron Burr (who was acquitted), Civil War abolitionist John Brown, and World War II spy Hans Max Haupt.

Additional Intel

In four seasons, actor Jude Ciccolella has appeared in fifty-eight episodes of 24 as Presidential advisor Mike Novick. Outside of the show, Ciccolella is also an accomplished singer and musician with four albums to his name.

3:00 pm - 4:00 pm

Director: Tim Iacofano
Writers: Howard Gordon & David Fury

Guest Cast: Julian Sands (Vladimir Bierko), Sean Astin (Lynn McGill), Jude Ciccolella (Mike Novick), Glenn Morshower (Agent Aaron Pierce), Kathleen Gati (Anya Suvarov)

"I'm not talking to a terrorist, you talk to them, you find out what he wants!" *President Charles Logan*

Timeframe   Key Events

3:00 P.M. Vladimir Bierko kills Erwich.
3:03 P.M. On the run, Nathanson calls an associate about Bierko.
3:04 P.M. A frantic McGill calls his sister to have her return the CTU key card that she stole.
3:06 P.M. McGill wants Jack arrested for disobeying orders.
3:08 P.M. Curtis takes away Jack's gun.
3:09 P.M. Audrey gets a call from Nathanson, who wants an untraced line to Jack in exchange for information about the gas.
3:10 P.M. Jack talks to Nathanson who admits he framed Jack, but now he needs protection and the gas stopped. They agree to meet.
3:11 P.M. Jack knocks out Curtis and drives to the meeting point.
3:18 P.M. McGill becomes suspicious of Audrey.
3:19 P.M. Audrey has Chloe wipe her phone records for the day.
3:20 P.M. Bierko calls Logan and demands the Suvarov motorcade route or he will release the Sentox nerve gas.
3:28 P.M. McGill shows Buchanan the call log.
3:30 P.M. Jack arrives at a phone booth and talks to Nathanson. A helicopter arrives with the terrorists.
3:33 P.M. Nathanson is surrounded, but Jack takes out the gunmen.
3:36 P.M. Another helicopter arrives and Nathanson is shot. Before he dies, he gives Jack a chip.
3:37 P.M. Audrey ignores a call from Jack because of McGill. She transfers the call to Chloe and Jack uploads the chip data.
3:42 P.M. Logan mulls his decision. Martha demands he remains firm.
3:46 P.M. Chloe needs Audrey's DoD password to decrypt the chip. McGill catches the move and accuses her of aiding Jack.
3:52 P.M. Chloe tells Jack the chip leads to a company called Omicron, run by Christopher Henderson. At McGill's orders, Buchanan is taken into custody.
3:54 P.M. Logan tells Novick to give Bierko the route.
3:58 P.M. Martha gets into the Suvarov limo.

Jack has to knock out Curtis.

McGill has Buchanan arrested.

Martha joins the Suvarovs for a ride.

President Charles Logan's alter-ego Greg Itzin says one of the great joys of the season for him was working again with Jean Smart, who plays Martha Logan. "Every time Jean and I did a scene it was always different," Itzin enthuses. "I always knew something was going to happen. I think it's safe to say that it was a great gift for both of us to have the other person be our wife or husband. We recognized it early on and we reveled in it. She's an amazingly available actress. She lives moment-to-moment and she doesn't make any plans that I can see. You work on a scene, like I go out on my porch the night before and put the scene in my head and figure out my actions and objectives. I don't just read the words; I figure out what he wants and why he's saying it

and then I kind of twist it. Like instead of being noble, I make him irritable, and that's what made Logan human to me. But when it comes to Jean, I'd make those plans and go in there and just end up playing anything that happens. We always moved moment-to-moment. Sometimes she would do things and I would go 'No', but in my mind I'm thinking 'Yes!' She wouldn't give me what I wanted but that would be perfect! One of my favorite scenes with her is the scene where she seduces me, because it's such a big, fat lie," he laughs. "And the scene where I go in and try to get her forgiveness, I loved that because there is no give in her at all!"

Research Files

Key Cards: Lynn McGill loses his key card, which provides him security access into CTU, when his sister steals it from him in an ambush. Key cards, also known as smart cards, are any small, plastic cards that have embedded integrated circuits that can provide data information. Smart cards usually have a security system that allows information on the card to remain encrypted until a card reader can decode the information. Examples of everyday uses would be hotel room 'keys' and ATM cards. The first data chip card was invented by German scientists Helmut Gröttrup and Jürgen Dethloff in 1968, but it wasn't until 1982 that the patent was established. Smart cards became more prevalent in the mid-nineties and have only risen in popularity with their use in SIM cards for mobile phones, debit cards, security access cards and more.

Additional Intel

Greg Itzin and Jean Smart worked together twenty years prior in the stage play, *Mrs. California*. Smart brought in a picture of them from that production and it was used as a set prop.

4:00 pm - 5:00 pm

Director: Tim Iacofano
Writers: Joel Surnow & Michael Loceff

Guest Cast: Peter Weller (Christopher Henderson), Kathleen Ga__ (Anya Suvarov), Nick Jameson (Yuri Suvarov), Julian Sands (Vladimir Bierko), Sean Astin (Lynn McGill)

(To Jack) "Just for the record, I never believed you were dead." Christopher Henderson

Timeframe — Key Events

4:00 P.M. Bierko prepares a missile to attack Suvarov's motorcade.

4:01 P.M. Logan realizes Martha is in the limo.

4:04 P.M. Logan calls Martha and orders her to get out but she hangs up on him.

4:08 P.M. Audrey and Chloe slip away to call Jack, who is on his way to Omicron. He reveals Henderson was his disgraced CTU recruiter.

4:18 P.M. Audrey and Chloe get Jack an appointment at Omicron.

4:20 P.M. Jack finds Henderson's office and has Audrey call his secretary to distract her.

4:21 P.M. Jack enters the office, but Henderson is waiting with a stun gun. Jack is revived and tells Henderson that the Sentox gas was created by his company.

4:23 P.M. Henderson denies any involvement. Jack demands to see where the nerve gas was made.

4:29 P.M. Edgar and Chloe advise McGill they are seeing chatter about the Suvarov route, but he dismisses them.

4:34 P.M. Curtis and Audrey agreed McGill is unfit.

4:39 P.M. McGill arrests Chloe and Edgar for unauthorized access, tries to throw Audrey out of CTU and orders guards to shoot Curtis if he draws his weapon. Curtis invokes the mental stability clause to remove McGill from command. Buchanan is reinstated.

4:46 P.M. Buchanan calls Logan about the Suvarov threat, but the President does nothing.

4:47 P.M. Agent Pierce is alerted of the attack and turns the car around. The terrorists launch a missile at the limo.

4:49 P.M. Logan is relieved everyone lived through the attack.

4:57 P.M. After a heated discussion, Henderson leaves Jack in the bunker. Realizing he's locked inside, Jack finds a bomb.

4:58 P.M. Henderson detonates the bomb from his car, but Jack is able to protect himself from the blast and escape.

4:59 P.M. Bierko calls Logan and says the country will pay for his duplicity.

Christopher Henderson greets Jack.

McGill is removed from command.

Bierko fires on the Suvarov limo.

In any given season, *24* shoots extensively on location in the greater Los Angeles area, using anything from highly recognizable landmarks to personal residences as a backdrop to the story. Locations manager John Johnston is part of the team in charge of matching the locations in the scripts to real-life places. For season five, Johnston says the team landed every location the producers wanted. "We've never been that stymied by locations ever. We did have a challenge with the Skirball Center, because it's really expensive to film there. I went to our producer with my hat in my hand going, 'Um... this is really expensive.' He said if it's what [the writers] want and has the look that the script asks for, do it. In reality, you don't find places like that for five and six

thousand dollars a day."

The Skirball Cultural Center in Los Angeles served as the location for Omicron International headquarters and Christopher Henderson's home. Set decorator Cloudia Rebar says whether she's at the studio or on location, she brings specific design principles to her set dressing. "For me, sets are about creating energy within the space with the furniture and the color and everything. The furniture helps describe the character even before he speaks, so it has to show his energy. I am a classical Feng Shui expert so I use it in an invisible way and I try to infuse every set with energy that you can actually tell is there. We did a house for Henderson at the Skirball Center, which was very beautiful and it showed a lot of sophistication and grace. But the house they said I had to use was all knotty pine and rather hokey. I walked in and wondered, 'How is this sophisticated and why would he be here?' There was a pool table in the kitchen, so I put a fancy top on it and some fancy high-back chairs to go around it like it was a breakfast nook. I took out as much as I could and brought in large-scale modern art to counteract the knotty pine and make it disappear. That was a challenge."

Research Files

Motorcade: The Suvarovs and Martha Logan ride in the Presidential limousine, which is targeted by Vladimir Bierko. The actual Presidential limousine looks deceptively plain, but in reality is a hand-crafted, reinforced vehicle created to withstand attack. The model is a Cadillac and was built by armored car specialists O'Gara, Hess, and Eisenhart. The interior of the vehicle is lined with five inches of ballistic armor, able to withstand anti-tank ballistics. The windows do not open for security purposes, which also allows the car to be environmentally sealed in case of a biological weapons attack. Secret Service refer to the vehicle as "Cadillac One", and the car is airlifted with the President to domestic and international locations by the Air Force. The first vehicle created for a President was the 1939 Lincoln V12 convertible for Franklin D. Roosevelt. Since that time, all Presidential limousines have either been Lincolns or Cadillacs.

Additional Intel

Early in the season, Jack's alias is revealed as Frank Flynn. EP Howard Gordon reveals novelist Vince Flynn helped the writers brainstorm at the start of the fifth season for a few weeks, so the name Flynn stuck in his head and was used.

5:00 pm - 6:00 pm

Director: Jon Cassar
Writer: Nicole Ranadive

Guest Cast: Peter Weller (Christopher Henderson), Kathleen Ga̶ (Anya Suvarov), Sean Astin (Lynn McGill), JoBeth Williams (Miriam Henderson), Glenn Morshower (Agent Aaron Pierce)

(To Henderson) "I shot her above the kneecap. She can still walk. You make me shoot her again; she'll be in a wheelchair for the rest of her life!" Jack Bauer

Timeframe   Key Events

5:00 P.M. Tony awakens and asks for Michelle.

5:02 P.M. Martha tells Pierce that Logan knew about the attack.

5:03 P.M. Bierko arms the canisters. His man, Ostroff, sets off to retrieve an important key card.

5:05 P.M. Ostroff coordinates to meet with McGill's sister to get the key card.

5:07 P.M. Jack calls CTU about Henderson's involvement and plans to go to his home.

5:09 P.M. On a terrorist's corpse, Curtis finds a schematic for the possible Sentox target.

5:11 P.M. Tony gets up and accesses a medical terminal, only to find out that Michelle is dead. He collapses in sorrow.

5:17 P.M. Martha and the Suvarovs return to the retreat. Logan is rebuffed by his wife.

5:23 P.M. Edgar determines the schematic is of a hospital. Inside, Bierko's man pushes a hidden gas canister on a gurney.

5:31 P.M. At the Henderson house, Jack surprises Miriam Henderson at gunpoint. He demands access to their computer.

5:32 P.M. Martha summons Agent Pierce and thanks him for saving her life.

5:35 P.M. Curtis arrives at the hospital.

5:41 P.M. Russian intelligence provides Bierko's name to Audrey as the financer of the attacks.

5:42 P.M. Chloe finds password protected phone numbers on Henderson's hard drive.

5:46 P.M. In the hospital basement, Curtis finds Bierko's man with an unlocked canister and shoots him dead.

5:53 P.M. Henderson arrives home and Jack threatens him. Miriam is shocked her husband has been lying to her. Jack shoots her in the knee to force Henderson to talk, but he refuses.

5:57 P.M. Curtis grabs the canister and runs it out to the sealed chemical truck before it detonates – saving the hospital and thousands of lives.

5:59 P.M. After killing Jenny and her boyfriend, Ostroff confirms to Bierko that he has the CTU key card.

Tony learns what happened to Michelle.

Jack shoots Henderson's wife.

Curtis runs with the Sentox.

In his second season on *24*, actor Roger Cross saw his character, Curtis Manning, get a bump up in responsibility as CTU Director of Field Operations. That meant Cross shot on location more, leading his team on various missions throughout the day, where he got to bond with his fellow commandos. "We have a core group of SWAT guys that we basically work with all season. We've all gotten to know each other and we play cards together and hang out; it's cool. We know our roles and we talk about it and they are really good at what they do. They know what we expect from them. They are just as committed and as integral as the rest of us, because without them doing a good job as the SWAT team it doesn't get the same feel as it should. It's great

working with them."

This episode featured one of Cross's favorite scenes of the season. "I really enjoyed the scene in the hospital where Curtis finally got to grab the canister and run it out of there. It was a heroic moment. Going in and saving the day worked out great because people thought for sure he was going to walk through that door and die. I got that response from a lot of people, 'Oh no, they're finally going to get Curtis!' Getting mail afterwards that said, 'We are so glad you are alive' was great," he laughs.

But executive producer Howard Gordon reveals Curtis almost did die in season five. "We were having trouble finding his place in the story, beyond being a field team functionary. He was really able to add great physical support and strength to those action sequences. But in terms of finding a dynamic for him, and someone to have a meaningful interaction with, it was hard for some reason."

Research Files

Buenos Aires: Christopher Henderson calls his bank in Buenos Aires for access to his safety deposit box. The capital of Argentina, Buenos Aires is located on the southeastern coast of South America. With more than eleven million people within its area, Buenos Aires is one of the ten most highly populated urban centers in the world. The city serves as the cultural and financial hub of Argentina, with one of the busiest ports in the world. Culturally, Buenos Aires is known for landmarks like one of the world's première opera houses, the Teatro Colón; the Botanical Gardens; and the Buenos Aires Zoo. The other major cultural claim to fame is the exotic dance known as the tango. Born in the brothels of the city, the dance was not seen as respectable until the Parisians eventually adopted it.

Additional Intel

All of the Fox News Channel broadcasts shown throughout the day on TV screens are actually produced by the *24* production team to run in the background to add to the sense of authenticity.

Chloe O'Brian

Experience:

CTU – Senior Analyst, Los Angeles Domestic Unit
CTU – Intelligence Agent, Los Angeles Domestic Unit
CTU – Internet Protocol Manager, Los Angeles Domestic Unit

Expertise:

Built IPSec architecture.
Attacks scripts, computer vulnerabilities, intrusion detection,
penetration testing, operational security, viruses.
Proficiency in Cerberus and PlutoPlus.

Education:

University of California (Davis) – Bachelor of Science,
Computer Science

Personal:

Divorced

Curtis Manning

Experience:

CTU – Director of Field Operations, Los Angeles
Domestic Unit
CTU – Assistant Director of Field Operations, Los
Angeles Domestic Unit
CTU – Assistant Director of Field Operations, Boston
Domestic Unit
CTU – Field Agent, Boston Domestic Unit
Boston PD – Special Weapons and Tactics

Education:

Basic SWAT School – MASD
University of Massachusetts – Bachelor of Arts,
Sociology

Military:

US Army – 2nd Infantry Brigade

Personal:

Single

6:00 pm - 7:00 pm

Director: Jon Cassar

Writers: Duppy Demetrius & Matt Michnovetz

Guest Cast: Elisha Cuthbert (Kim Bauer), C. Thomas Howell (Barry Landes), Sean Astin (Lynn McGill), Peter Weller (Christopher Henderson), Ray Wise (Hal Gardner)

(To Jack) "I'm happy you're alive. I am. But I can't give you what you need right now." *Kim Bauer*

Timeframe

Key Events

6:00 P.M. Ostroff reprograms McGill's CTU card with his image.

6:03 P.M. Buchanan tells Logan their only lead is Henderson.

6:04 P.M. Kim Bauer arrives at CTU with her fiancé, Barry.

6:05 P.M. Audrey alerts Jack about Kim.

6:06 P.M. Audrey drops the bomb on Kim that her father is alive.

6:08 P.M. Logan summons Vice President Hal Gardner to the retreat. To Novick's dismay but Logan's approval, the VP suggests martial law in LA.

6:11 P.M. At CTU, guards take Henderson, while Ostroff is cleared for entry.

6:18 P.M. Jack meets Kim, who is emotionally distant. Jack apologizes and tries to explain.

6:23 P.M. Tony begs Buchanan for the truth about Michelle. Relenting, Buchanan explains the Henderson connection.

6:25 P.M. Henderson is locked down in the interrogation room, but Jack knows his old mentor won't break easily.

6:26 P.M. Henderson is injected with extremely painful hyoscine-pentothal.

6:32 P.M. Novick tries to get Martha to help him talk sense into Logan.

6:35 P.M. Ostroff shuts down the ventilation system. A tech sees the problem and investigates.

6:37 P.M. The tech finds the canister and Ostroff kills her before she can sound an alert.

6:43 P.M. The canister is set to detonate.

6:45 P.M. McGill gets the bad news that his sister was murdered and he confesses to Buchanan she stole his key card.

6:47 P.M. The Ostroff key card breach is quickly found and CTU is put in lockdown.

6:52 P.M. Buchanan orders Jack to find the intruder.

6:56 P.M. Jack kills Ostroff. Buchanan orders an evacuation. The canister detonates.

6:57 P.M. Chloe is able to seal off a few rooms. Jack, Audrey, Kim and Barry make it into a sealed room, while Henderson is sealed into another room.

6:59 P.M. Edgar is too late and he dies before Chloe's eyes.

VP Hal Gardner joins Logan.

Kim Bauer faces her father.

Chloe watches in horror as Edgar meets a terrible fate.

This season saw many beloved *24* characters die, but none received the groundswell of fan ire like the death of Edgar Stiles. Louis Lombardi remembers when he was told by producers his character would die: "When they first said, 'We are going to do this,' I was like [*grimaces*]," the actor admits. "At first I was annoyed that I was dying. The show and the people are so great that you don't want to leave. It's like your family putting you up for adoption after two years! But I just trusted them. I read it and I was like, 'Holy cow! I'm not getting shot or strangled or thrown out of a plane or some kind of crazy killing.' This was a different way of going. When I read it, I was crying. I just felt that was the exact way it should be done. I didn't want to change anything, not a word or

a line. It was on the money: sad and heartbreaking. I thought, 'Wow, if you are going to die on TV, this is the way to go!' I kept telling people it would make television history. When it happened... it became television history."

For actress Mary Lynn Rajskub, shooting her scene through the glass was one of her hardest on the show. "I was really worried about doing the acting in that scene. I meant to sign up for a private acting coach, but because of my schedule I never got that to happen. But once we were shooting it was easy because it was really sad. I had also just gotten into a really big fight with somebody that I am no longer speaking to; so then I was just really upset for that. It was a good day for it. Generally, what I saw was the same thing that everyone else saw, which was his face out there and me being stuck in a room. It was *really* sad." Lombardi concurs, "It was a hard day. Everyone was sad the day I left. It was very nice and I really appreciate that whole group."

Research Files

Hyoscine-Pentothal: Christopher Henderson is injected with the "truth serum" hyoscine-pentothal in order to forcibly make him confess the details of where the Sentox gas is located. In reality, there is no such drug with the name hyoscine-pentothal, but there are truth-inducing agents separately known as hyoscine and pentothal. Hyoscine is a natural, highly toxic drug culled from plants known as nightshade. When mixed with morphine, it can cause amnesia in the victims. Alone, hyoscine has been found to reduce symptoms of depression and is extremely effective in combating the symptoms of sea sickness. Meanwhile, sodium pentothal is a barbiturate used during interrogations to get difficult subjects to open up and tell the truth. Once injected, it's been shown to depress the higher cortical functions in a human, making it harder for the complex function of lying to be effective. While the drug is considered helpful during interrogations, confessions made under it are often considered not entirely reliable because subjects with great mental control can still manipulate the truth.

Additional Intel

With the death of Edgar Stiles, the episode ends with the silent clock, which is used to honor the death of an important character. He is the only character to get the silent clock in season five.

7:00 pm - 8:00 pm

Director: Brad Turner

Writers: Joel Surnow & Michael Loceff

Guest Cast: Elisha Cuthbert (Kim Bauer), Stana Katic (Collette Stenger), Jayne Atkinson (Karen Hayes), Stephen Spinella (Miles Papazian), C. Thomas Howell (Barry Landes)

"You remember me? My name's Tony Almeida. You killed my wife Michelle Dessler this morning. She was my life, and you took her, and now I'm going to take yours." Tony Almeida

Timeframe	Key Events

7:03 P.M. A shocked Chloe is too stunned to work.

7:08 P.M. Distraught, Tony faces Henderson with a gun. Jack talks him down.

7:09 P.M. Agent Burke starts Henderson's injections again.

7:10 P.M. Logan and Gardner agree to have Homeland Security official Karen Hayes put in charge of CTU.

7:11 P.M. Gardner pushes Logan for martial law but the President is indecisive.

7:12 P.M. Bierko orders an associate to move all the gas to a new target.

7:18 P.M. An alarm tells Chloe that the door seals are breaking.

7:23 P.M. Chloe determines that she can flush the system with air conditioning, but she can't access the right terminal remotely. Jack offers to go to the computer.

7:30 P.M. Jack discovers iron bars block him from the computer room. He returns unsuccessful.

7:31 P.M. Chloe realizes the only other way in is from McGill's sealed space.

7:32 P.M. Jack calls McGill and explains the suicide mission. He accepts.

7:41 P.M. McGill runs out, turns off the computer program and returns to his space. Chloe starts the air conditioning.

7:43 P.M. McGill takes a few breaths and dies.

7:46 P.M. Jack asks Kim to stay and talk with him, but she admits she loves him but can't be around him anymore.

7:52 P.M. Martha tells Logan she still supports him, but not Gardner's initiatives.

7:53 P.M. Bierko calls Collette Stenger seeking schematics.

7:55 P.M. Karen calls Buchanan to tell him she is taking over.

7:56 P.M. Kim leaves with Barry.

7:57 P.M. Henderson goes into a coma and Tony prepares to get justice. Henderson wakes up and stabs a surprised Tony with the syringe. Henderson escapes.

7:59 P.M. Jack weeps for Tony.

McGill makes the ultimate sacrifice.

Kim and Jack have a sad goodbye.

Jack weeps for Tony.

While Jack's life has never a bed of roses, his broken relationship with his daughter, Kim Bauer, has been particularly heartbreaking over the five seasons. Their bond never recovered from Teri Bauer's death and Jack's continually dangerous line of work has only served to drive a deeper wedge between father and daughter. Yet Kim returns once more this year for a brief appearance at CTU, and Elisha Cuthbert admits she never expected to face her fictional dad again. "I left at the end of the third season and didn't come back for the fourth and thought I would be done forever. I didn't expect to be back on the show again. When they called me and we talked about it, I was sort of like, 'Am I going to be able to do this?' I was actually

really afraid. I thought [Kim] was gone and I wouldn't find her again."

Audiences have always had a love/hate relationship with Kim, so Cuthbert wanted to make sure that her character came back in a strong way. "We had some serious [talks]," she reveals. "There was writing and re-writing and then back and forth and faxing each other things trying to make it great. I have gotten a lot of flack from critics and that's fine because to me, if I can do anything, it's just to make them feel something, whether it's excited or on the edge of your seat going, 'What is she doing?' It's all fine to me as long as it comes from a real place. But initially, [the story] was her getting in peril again and I said, 'We can't do that. If I'm going to come back, I'm not going to put the audience through that sort of misery.' But then we found a great reason to come back, and not knowing [Jack] is alive and discovering all of that is really cool stuff to play with. It made for good stuff on the show and between Jack and I again. I think season five was probably the best season out of all of them."

Research Files

Martial Law: President Charles Logan and Vice President Hal Gardner discuss the possibility of instituting martial law on the area of Los Angeles in order to help the search for the Sentox gas. Martial law is the rule instituted by the military in order to control the population during times of war, extreme natural disasters or military takeover. In more autocratic governments, martial law is used as a tool to help quell civil unrest or to impose government policy on the populace. In the United States, it's very difficult to impose martial law because of the 1878 Posse Comitatus Act, which forbids military intervention of domestic law enforcement. Classic example of its rare use include US General Andrew Jackson's call for martial law in New Orleans in 1812, Hawaii's martial law imposition during World War II from 1941 to 1945, and most recently, the lockdown of New Orleans after Hurricane Katrina.

Additional Intel

Many fans were upset that Tony did not get a silent clock, which often honors a major character's [departure from] the show. EP Howard Gordon says, "I don't know why we didn't give him the clock. I think part of it was the nature of the [departure], but there was no conscious reason."

8:00 pm - 9:00 pm

Director: Brad Turner
Story: Sam Montgomery
Teleplay: Howard Gordon & Evan Katz

Guest Cast: Stephen Spinella (Miles Papazian), Jayne Atkinson (Karen Hayes), Julian Sands (Vladimir Bierko), Ray Wise (Hal Gardner), DB Woodside (Wayne Palmer)

(To Miles) "I'll pay for your dry cleaning."
Chloe O'Brian

Timeframe   Key Events

8:00 P.M. Chloe decrypts Collette Stenger's name on Henderson's computer.

8:04 P.M. Logan tells the press LA is under a military curfew.

8:05 P.M. Karen and Miles arrive at CTU.

8:07 P.M. Miles takes Chloe's key card and settles at Edgar's station.

8:09 P.M. Wayne Palmer calls Agent Pierce and asks to meet him.

8:12 P.M. Collette calls Bierko and says she is on her way with the schematics for the next target.

8:17 P.M. Karen and Buchanan lock horns and she admits CTU is being absorbed by Homeland Security.

8:22 P.M. Curtis and Jack arrive at Collette's hotel but they only find her lover, Stoller, an undercover German Federal Intelligence Service operative. He refuses to blow his cover by revealing her whereabouts. Jack takes him into custody.

8:28 P.M. Collette arrives at Bierko's safe house.

8:30 P.M. Jack talks to Stoller alone and offers him the highly coveted US WET list in exchange for her location.

8:31 P.M. Jack calls Chloe for the list but she can't get it without her key card.

8:32 P.M. Chloe hatches a scheme to dump coffee on Miles. While he's gone, she gets her card and uploads the list to Jack's PDA.

8:33 P.M. Miles returns suspicious of Chloe. Stoller confirms the list is legit and says he is supposed to meet Collette at Van Nuys Airport.

8:43 P.M. Karen and Miles ambush Chloe about the WET list. Karen calls Jack and she is forced to let him proceed.

8:46 P.M. Collette and Stoller meet in the parking lot.

8:47 P.M. Collette realizes she's been betrayed and is arrested.

8:55 P.M. Collette demands immunity for her information.

8:57 P.M. Wayne is accosted by a black van that runs him off the road. He escapes into the woods.

8:58 P.M. Collette reveals her schematics came from Audrey.

Karen and Miles arrive at CTU.

Collette is taken into custody.

Wayne Palmer is run off the road.

Executive producer Howard Gordon admits that Tony's death wasn't as dramatically satisfying as expected. "I was extremely happy with the way Kiefer underscored Tony's death, but less happy with the way he died. It didn't have the impact that I hoped it would have. There was a moment that Kiefer played where he let out a primal scream, which we wound up cutting. I really liked it, but we decided it might be too much. It was a great moment that underscored how much this character meant to Jack and I hope it turns up as a DVD extra someday."

Later on when Karen Hayes first walks into CTU with Miles Papazian, the stage is seemingly set for the familiar scenario of outsiders coming into CTU with an agenda and an attitude. But

the writers and actress Jayne Atkinson turn that assumption on its head as the season evolves. Early on though, Atkinson heard lots of disparaging remarks from critics and fans about Karen's direct demeanor. "Oh, people say, 'She's a bitch' and all kinds of things, like a strong woman just needs to get in the sack with someone," she laughs. "I have never played a part where I knew I wasn't going to be liked before, so it was an interesting journey for me as an actor; honestly, it was fun. I always play the nice one that everyone loves and wants to be nurtured by. That's not this part and so I like playing a woman who is negotiating power. She is using her feeling and her intellect together and she's willing to not be liked. She's not emotional, but not afraid to express her emotion. I got right up in Jack's face and no one has done that. I felt like it was important for me to use the power of emotion and expression." What Atkinson says also helped swing audiences in her eventual favor was portraying the intelligence of Karen and her clear appraisal of all sides in the crisis. "She gets in there and eventually realizes, 'Wait a minute, they are really handling things.' It's important that I portrayed her as somebody who can think on her feet like that."

Research Files

WET List: To get to Collette Stenger, Jack offers Stoller access to the highly secretive US WET (Western European Terrorist) list — a fictional list of known terrorists in the Western hemisphere. In reality, such lists exist and are maintained and investigated by the US government agency known as the National Counterterrorism Center (NCTC). The agency initially started about two years after September 11, 2001 as the Terrorist Threat Integration Center (TTIC) and was renamed (NCTC) and reorganized with the Intelligence Reform and Terrorism Prevention Act of 2004. The department's primary functions are to analyze terrorism intelligence and "chatter", create terrorism information databases, and support and plan US counterterrorism activities. The NCTC list is made up from data collected in the department and with additional intelligence provided by the CIA, the FBI and the National Security Agency (NSA).

Additional Intel

Writer Sam Montgomery joined *24* as a producer for its fifth season. An accomplished screenwriter, Montgomery worked with director Jonathan Mostow writing the films, *U-571* and *Breakdown*.

9:00 pm - 10:00 pm

Director: Jon Cassar
Writer: David Ehrman

Guest Cast: Peter Weller (Christopher Henderson), Kate Mara (Shari Rothenberg), DB Woodside (Wayne Palmer), Jayne Atkinson (Karen Hayes), Julian Sands (Vladimir Bierko)

> "The only thing that got me through this was that I knew you would come. I knew you would come."
> Audrey Raines

Timeframe — Key Events

9:00 P.M. Buchanan has Chloe covertly investigate Audrey.

9:01 P.M. Audrey is taken into custody.

9:02 P.M. Collette is escorted into CTU.

9:04 P.M. Jack comes up against Karen and demands a chance to talk to Audrey first.

9:07 P.M. Bierko and company ambush some cops for their uniforms and vehicle.

9:08 P.M. Chloe finds out Audrey and Cummings stayed in the same hotel room one night.

9:15 P.M. Audrey tells an angry Jack she had nothing to do with Collette. Jack reveals the Cummings connection and she admits she slept with him, but that was all.

9:19 P.M. Karen assigns Agent Burke to torture Audrey.

9:21 P.M. Jack refuses to allow the torture to happen. He is tasered and handcuffed.

9:26 P.M. Wayne is chased by Henderson's men.

9:27 P.M. Agent Pierce goes to look for Wayne.

9:28 P.M. Jack implores Karen to let him focus on the real culprit, Collette. Jack enlists Chloe's help.

9:31 P.M. Bierko arrives at the Wilshire Gas Company, where they bring the canisters to the main distribution tanks.

9:39 P.M. Pierce finds Wayne and they run from the gunmen.

9:40 P.M. Chloe finds calls from Collette to Henderson, nullifying her immunity.

9:41 P.M. Jack runs into Collette's cell and pulls a gun on her until she admits Henderson fed her Audrey's name and the schematic is for a natural gas distribution center.

9:43 P.M. Jack stops Audrey's torture.

9:46 P.M. Pierce fires on the gunmen. He and Wayne escape.

9:52 P.M. Jack and Curtis chopper to Wilshire, while Bierko sets up the canisters. Jack and Curtis overtake Bierko's men.

9:56 P.M. Bierko activates the canisters. Jack runs to ignite the pipelines so the Sentox is incinerated before it leaves the plant.

9:58 P.M. Jack and Bierko fight as the plant explodes in a ball of flame.

Jack saves Audrey.

Pierce and Wayne are attacked.

Jack runs from the exploding plant.

Determining whether or not Audrey Raines is a traitor is the emotional center of this episode with Jack squaring off against two strong women: Karen Hayes and Audrey herself. Jayne Atkinson says one her favorite moments occurs when she is arguing with Jack about torturing Audrey. "There was a moment with Kiefer, but it didn't end up on screen, that was really beautiful, where he says, 'We have to focus on the right priorities.' It was so moving. It completely changed the way I spoke to him. Instead of yelling at him, I said, 'I know what's important.' It was this tremendous human moment between two people who had to negotiate power."

Later on, Kim Raver cites Jack's actual, brutal interrogation of

Audrey as her favorite. "It was one of those acting days that you wait for. We were allowed to do just that scene the whole day, which is really unheard of. It was a three- or four-page scene and normally we do eight pages a day, but I think Jon Cassar and Kiefer knew the importance of that scene. It was so multi-layered and there was so much at stake. There were so many things going on: is she telling the truth or is she not telling the truth, which is very *24*-esque, but also they had a relationship and there is this sexual tension. There is trust and distrust. How do you build the trust again? Also just working with Kiefer, it's so extraordinary to work with as talented an actor as someone like Kiefer. In those moments, you really see the difference between him and other actors. We'd be off laughing or he'd be playing chess and then we'd come on and I could see in his eyes, he hears 'action' and he's right in it. It was a very intense moment when he had to push the table and grab my throat and push me up against the wall."

Research Files

Sexual Harassment Charge: Wacky CTU tech Shari Rothenberg reveals that she brought Miles up on sexual harassment charges. First coined at Cornell University in 1974, sexual harassment is considered a form of illegal discrimination in many countries and includes everything from minor offenses all the way up to rape and forced sexual encounters. The US Equal Employment Opportunity Commission says an average of 15,000 sexual harassment cases are reported annually stemming from workplace violations. The majority of reports (anywhere from forty to sixty percent) are filed by women against male coworkers. In the US, the Civil Rights Act of 1964 Title VII prohibits employment discrimination based on race, sex (both male and female), national origin or religion. While many cases are filed, very few make it to federal court and the cases are often settled between the parties.

Additional Intel

During the season, Mary Lynn Rajskub was able to take a few days to appear in her director friend Jonathan Dayton's indie film, *Little Miss Sunshine*, as Pageant Assistant Pam. The film went on to win two Academy Awards.

10:00 pm - 11:00 pm

Director: Jon Cassar

Writers: Manny Coto & Sam Montgomery

Guest Cast: Peter Weller (Christopher Henderson), Kate Mara (Shari Rothenberg), Stephen Spinella (Miles Papazian), Ray Wise (Hal Gardner), Sandrine Holt (Evelyn)

> "These are the people who killed my brother, Jack. They shot him with a bullet right through his neck and then he died in my arms. Put yourself in my position. Could you just walk away?" Wayne Palmer

Timeframe	Key Events

10:00 P.M. Jack emerges with Bierko's unconscious body. Curtis confirms the Sentox is destroyed.

10:03 P.M. Jack calls Buchanan and confirms that Henderson was working for someone else.

10:04 P.M. The VP tells Karen to move forward with the takeover. Miles suggests they get Audrey to speak against Buchanan.

10:07 P.M. At the retreat, Wayne tells Pierce that Evelyn was David's informant inside the White House.

10:09 P.M. Wayne and Pierce confront Evelyn, who admits her daughter has been kidnapped by people who want evidence of the conspiracy.

10:18 P.M. Wayne calls Jack about Evelyn.

10:19 P.M. Audrey reads a statement written by Miles that says she blames Buchanan for mishandling the crisis. She refuses to sign it.

10:21 P.M. Jack calls Audrey, she explains the take-over of CTU. He asks her and Chloe to get sat tracking of the meeting place.

10:22 P.M. Audrey tells Karen she will sign if Chloe is assigned to her.

10:23 P.M. Henderson holds Evelyn's daughter hostage.

10:29 P.M. A surprised Gardner sees Wayne and Pierce.

10:33 P.M. Evelyn and Wayne connect. She says she is terrified she caused Palmer's death. Henderson calls her cell. Jack is secretly patched in and the meeting point is given.

10:41 P.M. Jack meets Wayne and Evelyn. Chloe sends the sat view of the location to his PDA.

10:46 P.M. Evelyn drives to meet Henderson, while Jack and Wayne approach by foot.

10:57 P.M. Henderson gives Evelyn her daughter. Jack and Wayne open fire. Henderson escapes in her car.

10:58 P.M. Evelyn is shot and she says the VP is not involved.

10:59 P.M. Henderson calls President Logan, who assures him Jack and Wayne will die.

Evelyn is reunited with her daughter.

Evelyn is hit in the gun fight.

Logan is revealed as the orchestrator.

The climactic explosion of the gas plant ranks as one of the most impressive action sequences ever created for the series. Making the sequence come to life started with finding the right location, which happened to be at a plant in Redondo Beach, California.

Key assistant for locations, Tristan Daoussis remembers their department dealt with a list of unexpected problems leading to the shoot day. "What was so funny about that was a newspaper released that we were going to be down there, so we had this influx of people. So late in the evening at the shoot, we had a large group of fans assembled to watch and that's not what you want with the pyrotechnics and stunts! We also sent out a flyer to

the neighborhood with a typo so it said, 'You should be alarmed' instead of 'You should *not* be alarmed,'" he laughs.

DP Rodney Charters cites the sequence with Kiefer running from the plant as it blows up behind him as one of his visual highlights of the entire season. "It was great because it looked like a big feature. When Kiefer runs down this long line of exploding flames, it stands out. We tracked that with a little golf cart, with camera operator Guy Skinner handholding [the camera] and we ran just ahead of Kiefer. There were precisely timed gas explosions that were so well timed that when Kiefer got to the end, his back was almost on fire." Special effects gurus, Stan and Scott Blackwell chuckle and concur. "It was a cold night at the beach and when Kiefer was done running, he was steaming! We asked him how he was and he said, 'I'm hot!' We had six liquid propane mortars and they stacked it up on a 100 mil lens, so it looks like he is right there. When it first went off, they also wanted the valves to blow off, so that was an interesting gag to come up with. We finished with the big tanks blowing up, which was cool. It was a busy night!"

Research Files

Department of Homeland Security (DHS): Karen announces to CTU that they are being absorbed by DHS, which will continue to oversee the recovery mission. The DHS is a cabinet-level department of the federal government of the United States created by President George W. Bush after the 9/11 attacks. Tasked with protecting the civilian population by preventing or dealing with domestic-soil emergencies, DHS is primarily focused on terrorism. Since its inception, DHS introduced the color-coded terrorism risk advisory scale, which alerts citizens of the threat level within the nation. The DHS is the third largest cabinet department in the federal government, with almost 200,000 employees across the nation.

Additional Intel

While NASCAR Nextel Cup driver Carl Edwards was in California for the Auto Club 500, he stopped by the *24* set to film an uncredited appearance as Homeland Security agent Jim Hill.

11:00 pm - 12:00 am

Director: Brad Turner
Writer: David Fury

Guest Cast: DB Woodside (Wayne Palmer), Glenn Morshower (Agent Aaron Pierce), Jayne Atkinson (Karen Hayes), Peter Weller (Christopher Henderson), William Devane (James Helle

> "I just spoke with Jack. Gardner isn't the one who's behind this. It's President Logan." Audrey Raines

Timeframe

Key Events

11:00 P.M. Evelyn explains she hid a tape of Logan and Henderson in a safety deposit box. She gives Jack the key.

11:02 P.M. Jack calls Audrey and asks her to involve her father and get out of CTU.

11:05 P.M. Cleaned up, Jack and Wayne leave Evelyn and her daughter at a motel.

11:08 P.M. Logan calls Karen issuing a warrant for Jack in the murder of Palmer. It's to be CTU's priority.

11:11 P.M. Audrey is ready to leave and lies to Karen about not speaking to Jack.

11:12 P.M. Karen orders a transponder be put on Audrey's car.

11:19 P.M. Jack and Wayne break into the bank manager's home and demand he takes them to the bank.

11:20 P.M. Audrey calls Heller, who is on a plane. He changes routes to meet her.

11:22 P.M. At a gas station, Audrey calls Chloe, who tells her to sweep her car. The transponder is found and Audrey places it on another vehicle.

11:23 P.M. Gardner angrily confronts Logan about the warrant for Jack.

11:25 P.M. Evelyn falls and her daughter calls 911.

11:27 P.M. Henderson gets the 911 alert and heads to the motel.

11:33 P.M. At the bank, Jack gets a call from Pierce about the warrant. Jack reveals that Logan is behind everything.

11:34 P.M. Karen realizes they lost Audrey.

11:38 P.M. Henderson shoots Evelyn's paramedic. He demands Jack's location.

11:47 P.M. Jack plays Evelyn's tape, which is Henderson's confession to Logan.

11:50 P.M. Henderson's men surround the bank. The manager trips the silent alarm.

11:55 P.M. Chloe scrambles Miles' sat track of Audrey.

11:58 P.M. The LAPD arrive and a shootout ensues. The manager is shot but they are able to get to a police car.

11:59 P.M. The manager dies. Audrey is at the airport waiting for her father.

Audrey gets Heller involved.

Chloe helps Audrey.

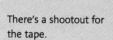

There's a shootout for the tape.

Olivier Benamou is one of two graphic artists that work full-time creating the screen animations seen on the monitors in any given episode. What looks to a viewer like standard software on a computer screen, a password input page or even the CTU database pages, are all created from scratch as called for by the script. "The way we start a season is by creating the background package, which is a bunch of animated screens that aren't particularly relevant to any story. As the season progresses, we are called to do very specific tasks. For instance, if Chloe is doing a satellite sweep, obviously, that has to be built because NASA is not going to give us that access, unfortunately," Benamou smiles. "I also work with some props because

of product placements, like Jack is using a Treo PDA, so we have to put animations on that PDA. He may ask Chloe to send him something, so the animation on her monitor will eventually turn up on his PDA too."

As with the other departments, graphics also has a very short period to create their pieces of the *24* puzzle. Benamou explains, "We shoot two episodes at a time, so the amount of time we have to create the animations is very short. On a feature, you'll have three or four months to create an animation. I'm lucky if I get three or four days to turn something around. Since *24* is based per-hour, you can't have the same animation from hour one to hour two. Every episode has something different. What we do is try to take the concept of what a CIA organization would be like and make it more lively and interesting with bells and whistles. I create it all in Adobe Photoshop, Studio Max 3D, Adobe After Effects and I animate in Director."

Research Files

Safety Deposit Boxes: Evelyn reveals to Jack and Wayne that the evidence tape against Logan is located in a safety deposit box in a bank. Safety deposit boxes have long been offered by banks as a way for customers to protect valuables like money, bonds, jewelry, personal mementos and highly valuable items. The box is made of several layers of metal with an end that opens by a secured lock. These boxes reside inside a secured storage container, often inside a vault. The boxes have been designed to be impenetrable to fire and burglary. Locks on contemporary safety deposit boxes can either be standard, with a key lock, or they can be electronic. High-end banks will often augment their deposit box security with biometric measures, such as fingerprint or retinal scans from a customer, to ensure security breaches cannot be made.

Additional Intel

Originally actress Laurie Metcalf (*Roseanne, Desperate Housewives*) was cast as Karen Hayes, but the producers and the actress mutually agreed to part ways.

Bill Buchanan

Experience:

CTU – Special Agent in Charge,
    Los Angeles Domestic Unit
Division – Associate Special Agent in Charge,
    Los Angeles Office
Division – Senior Agent, Seattle Office
Division – Intelligence Analyst, Seattle Office
CTU – Agent, New York Domestic Unit

Education:

Brown University – Bachelor of Arts, English

Personal:

Single

Audrey Raines

Experience:

Department of Defense – Inter-Agency Liaison
Department of Defense, Washington DC
    – Senior Policy Analyst
Anderson Aerospace Corporation
    – Consultant for Government Contracts
Ballard Technology – Government Liaison
Registered Lobbyist
US Congress House Armed Services Committee
    – Legislative Assistant

Education:

Brown University – Master of Arts, Public Policy
Yale University – Bachelor of Arts, English

Personal:

Spouse – Paul Raines (deceased)

12:00 am - 1:00 am

Director: Brad Turner

Writer: Howard Gordon

Guest Cast: DB Woodside (Wayne Palmer), Jude Ciccolella (Mike Novick), Glenn Morshower (Agent Aaron Pierce), Peter Weller (Christopher Henderson), William Devane (James Heller)

(To Logan) "Your chair is not a throne."

James Heller

Timeframe　　　　　　　Key Events

12:04 A.M. Jack and Wayne wait for Buchanan. Jack leaves to meet Heller and Wayne goes with Buchanan.

12:07 A.M. Heller lands and Jack explains he's been framed.

12:08 A.M. Jack plays the tape for Audrey and Heller. Jack asks them to present the tape to the Attorney General.

12:10 A.M. Heller arrests Jack and Audrey. He thinks he can get Logan to quietly step down.

12:17 A.M. Karen and Miles set Chloe up in a sting. She calls the airfield and Karen deploys agents. Chloe is arrested.

12:18 A.M. Karen calls Logan, who says he will send the military. The President instead calls Henderson.

12:19 A.M. Karen calls Novick.

12:22 A.M. Novick confirms with Gardner and an LA General that Logan called neither of them about Bauer.

12:23 A.M. Novick confronts Logan.

12:30 A.M. Miles locks up Chloe but not before she pickpockets his key card to escape.

12:31 A.M. Chloe grabs a laptop and runs.

12:33 A.M. Heller calls Logan.

12:35 A.M. Logan calls Henderson about Heller.

12:40 A.M. Martha tells Pierce she is concerned about Logan. Pierce asks her to meet him at the stables and he will explain it all.

12:41 A.M. Heller confronts Logan. He demands the President step down and calls Gardner to witness the resignation.

12:45 A.M. Chloe arrives at Buchanan's home and sets up her laptop.

12:46 A.M. At the stable, Martha only finds Pierce's cell.

12:47 A.M. Jack is able to melt off his restraints and cut Audrey free.

12:52 A.M. Henderson's black ops team arrives. Jack gets the tape back.

12:54 A.M. Henderson grabs Audrey, cuts her artery and demands the tape. Jack provides it and Henderson escapes.

12:57 A.M. Henderson calls Logan, who is able to turn the tables on Heller. Secret Service removes Heller from the retreat.

Heller confronts Logan.

Martha finds Pierce's abandoned cell phone.

Audrey is cut by Henderson.

For the role of Jack's former mentor and season-long nemesis, the *24* producers brought in respected character actor Peter Weller for the role of Christopher Henderson. A personal friend of producers Surnow, Gordon and Coto, Weller took on the role and worked with the writers to help shape Henderson's ultimate purpose as the season progressed. "The guy was an ultra-patriot and he definitely had a vision about how the world should go," he says of his character. "He definitely had a view about how and where America should play. I based him somewhat on Air Force General Curtis LeMay and the John Birch Society folks of the Cold War days. LeMay was an almost reactionary Chief Of Staff for the Air Force back in the Kennedy era and held with nuking Cuba and/or

Russia during the missile crisis. Many folks believe LeMay was right, just as many probably believe Henderson and his ultra-American philosophy is the right way to go. I'm sure that there are a few folks roaming around who think Christopher Henderson had it right."

The producers admit the original plan was to have Tony Almeida kill Henderson in CTU, but after some discussion they decided that Henderson had more of a story to explore. Weller says his argument for Henderson to the producers was, "If you've got an interesting and dynamic guy like this, who has all these textured ideals about where America should go, don't turn him into some sort of a crackpot. So they fleshed him out further and it was very satisfying to say lines like 'And I'm not talking about the op-ed page in the *New York Times*, Jack!' Henderson definitely believed America should dance a stronger dance in world affairs. I also don't think that Henderson's position was so much different from Jack's stance. Jack would have never had gotten into [Henderson's business] had the former President not been shot; thus it became a personal vendetta."

Research Files

Brachial Artery: Christopher Henderson ups the stakes when he cuts the artery in Audrey's arm. The brachial artery is the primary blood vessel of the upper arm, running from the shoulder to the elbow. There are several branches off the artery and they serve to provide blood to the biceps and triceps. The pulse of the artery can be found in the anterior of the elbow, which can be read with a stethoscope. Artery injuries are particularly dangerous because the strength of the bleeding can quickly become life threatening. Doctors recommend immediately applying pressure to any severe bleeding to stem the flow until medical attention can be found. Tourniquets are not recommended as they can contribute to necrosis, or the death of cells, making them unable to heal.

Additional Intel

Season five of *24* had the highest ratings of any season with an average of 13.8 million viewers. In the US, the season was ranked at number twenty-three for 2005-2006.

1:00 am - 2:00 am

Director: Dwight Little
Writers: Steve Mitchell & Craig Van Sickle

Guest Cast: William Devane (James Heller), Peter Weller (Christopher Henderson), Stephen Spinella (Miles Papazian), Paul McCrane (Graem), Jayne Atkinson (Karen Hayes)

(To Buchanan) "I hope you don't mind me bossing you around, but technically, I don't work for you anymore."
Chloe O'Brian

Timeframe

1:00 A.M. Audrey is stable. Heller calls and says Logan failed to resign.
1:02 A.M. Jack calls Buchanan and Chloe, who starts tracking Henderson.
1:06 A.M. Henderson tells Logan that Jack is alive.
1:07 A.M. Chloe finds Henderson.
1:08 A.M. Jack runs Henderson off the road and they start shooting.
1:09 A.M. Out of ammo, Henderson says if he dies, Heller dies.
1:10 A.M. Jack calls Heller, who confirms a helicopter is following him.
1:11 A.M. Heller refuses to be a pawn for Logan, so he drives his car off a cliff into a lake. The helicopter leaves.
1:12 A.M. Jack beats on Henderson, who refuses to give the location of the tape. Audrey tells Jack to kill him.
1:18 A.M. Logan calls a mysterious man named Graem and wants to "cancel the action".
1:20 A.M. An agent tells Martha that Logan wants to see her. She's locked in an empty room and she panics.
1:21 A.M. On sat, Chloe determines Henderson met another car and it went back to the airport.
1:22 A.M. Jack calls Curtis to retrieve Audrey and Henderson. Jack races to the airport.
1:29 A.M. Karen and Miles are alerted that Chloe escaped.
1:31 A.M. Logan goes to Martha and admits his guilt. He begs her not to expose him. Sickened, she agrees.
1:44 A.M. Jack arrives at the airfield. Chloe says the chopper is heading towards Audrey.
1:45 A.M. Jack calls Audrey. She refuses to leave and threatens to shoot Henderson.
1:46 A.M. Curtis arrives, saves Audrey and arrests Henderson.
1:48 A.M. Jack sneaks onto the airfield.
1:55 A.M. Miles tracks Chloe down.
1:57 A.M. Karen calls Buchanan to warn Chloe.
1:59 A.M. Jack enters the cargo bay of the plane before it takes off.

Key Events

Heller drives off the road.

Graem comes into the picture.

Jack boards the mystery plane.

Of Heller's dramatic plunge off a cliff into the depths, William Devane reveals that he always knew his character survived. "We shot a scene where I climbed out of the water, but they never showed it. [The producers] did have it, but they figured they could leave it up in the air because it became an interesting question as Heller was somewhat popular." With three seasons' worth of appearances on *24*, Devane says he's always happy to get the call from the writers that Heller is needed again. "It's fun to do. Working with Kiefer is a great experience. He is the hardest working guy I've ever worked with. It's been a really positive experience in every way. I've got nothing to bitch about," he says with his trademark grin.

This episode also gives audiences their first taste of Bill Buchanan outside of CTU. James Morrison says, "I would have to say some of my favorite scenes were the ones with Chloe in my house. And it's always nice to be able to say exactly what you are thinking to someone. Buchanan can't do that very often because he's a patriot and a bureaucrat. There's a hierarchy and you can't break that. He's also a polite person with manners, he's a gentleman, but to be able to call Miles an ass-kisser was a truly enjoyable moment."

On a more serious note, Morrison says bringing down a President was sad. "I think part of having a job like this, as an actor on *24*, but also as Buchanan at CTU, is that nothing surprises you. Even the corruption and the deception at the highest levels of government, it just doesn't surprise me. I don't think it's a jaded thing. But at the same time, the evil that man is capable of never ceases to amaze me; you're just dumbstruck by it. Yet, there's the other side of you that just knows they are capable of it, why should it surprise? That's why there is no celebration at the end with the undoing of the President. There's no satisfaction in seeing our country have to suffer what it's about to suffer."

Research Files

Van Nuys Airport: Chloe discovers that an associate of Henderson's is returning to Van Nuys Airport and Jack follows in pursuit. The actual Van Nuys Airport is a non-commercial airport that only operates private, chartered flights or local news helicopters. Surprisingly, it is the world's busiest general aviation airport, despite its lack of standard commercial flights, operating an average of 1,400 flights per day. The airport is also a popular set for film shooting, with the series *Airwolf*, *Alias* and the classic films, *Casablanca* and *American Beauty*, all lensing there at one time or another. Van Nuys Airport began way back in 1928 as Metropolitan Airport. In 1942, the airport was bought by the US government and turned into a primary military base that was used extensively during World War II. After the war, in 1949, the city of Los Angeles bought the airport for one dollar and renamed it the San Fernando Valley Airport. It received its final name change in 1957.

Additional Intel

From this episode forward, Kiefer Sutherland was credited as an executive producer of *24*. The new title came with his Fox deal to remain on the series for three more years and start his own development company, East Side Entertainment.

2:00 am - 3:00 am

Director: Dwight Little
Writers: Joel Surnow & Michael Loceff

Guest Cast: Stephen Spinella (Miles Papazian), Paul McCrane (Graem), Jayne Atkinson (Karen Hayes), Jude Ciccolella (Mike Novick), Andrew Hawkes (Scott Evans)

(To Miles) "You have no idea what you're dealing with, you little ass-kisser." Bill Buchanan

Timeframe

Key Events

2:00 A.M. Buchanan briefs Karen on Jack.

2:03 A.M. Buchanan sends Chloe to a nearby hotel.

2:04 A.M. Homeland Security arrives at Buchanan's and Karen orders him to be brought to CTU.

2:06 A.M. Chloe calls Karen for help accessing the flight manifest.

2:07 A.M. In cargo, Jack gets a call from Chloe, who explains Karen's support. Chloe gets Jack the air marshal's seat number.

2:09 A.M. Jack knocks out the marshal and takes his gun.

2:14 A.M. Chloe alerts Jack to Hans Meyer, an associate of Henderson's at Omicron.

2:15 A.M. Jack lures Hans into the galley, knocks him out and puts him in cargo.

2:24 A.M. The air marshal awakens and the pilot is alerted. He prepares to turn the plane around.

2:31 A.M. Jack searches Hans' luggage to no avail. Jack is sealed inside cargo.

2:33 A.M. Cargo starts to depressurize. Chloe calls Karen, who connects Jack to the pilot.

2:34 A.M. Jack tells the pilot and co-pilot he is a federal agent, but they don't believe him.

2:35 A.M. Jack shorts some wires which cause the plane to lurch. Afraid, the pilot restores air and opens cargo.

2:37 A.M. Jack demands the pilot circle so he can search the plane.

2:38 A.M. Logan freaks about Jack hijacking the plane and calls Graem.

2:44 A.M. Buchanan is led back into CTU.

2:48 A.M. Logan calls Karen and says he wants Jack, dead or alive.

2:49 A.M. Novick is dismayed and tries to reason with Logan.

2:54 A.M. Chloe discovers that the co-pilot used to fly for Omicron.

2:55 A.M. Chloe tells Jack and then Jack tells the pilot. The suspicious co-pilot knocks the pilot out.

2:57 A.M. Jack storms the cockpit, socks the co-pilot and gets the tape back.

2:59 A.M. Graem demands Logan shoot down the plane.

Chloe handles a problem.

The co-pilot gives Jack the tape.

Graem tells Logan to shoot the plane down.

Co-creator Robert Cochran explains that the shadow group, led by the mysterious Graem (Paul McCrane), seen pulling Logan's strings in the last third of the season came out of a need to ratchet up the story tension leading into the finale. "Part of it as a storyteller is that you are always looking for another layer. There is a man behind the curtain and then there is a man behind the man behind the curtain, and you just keep going. I also think realistically everybody knows the way politics works and that politicians are not all powerful by any means. They have people they have to answer to that put them in office. That's been true with every President in this century and probably with every President we've ever had, except for the first

couple. In this century with the rise of corporations, it's a fact of life. All the Presidents have constituents that they have to please, whether it's corporations or special interest groups. So if you are looking for who's behind him, there are these people who also give Logan more pressure. If you have a villain that has nothing to worry about or we make things too easy for him, it's not as interesting. But we have a guy who is the villain [Logan] and on the one hand, you have Jack Bauer who's suspicious and coming after him; and on the other hand, there are the guys who put Logan where he is and they expect him to do certain things. If they are mad at him, too, it increases the pressure on him. Watching Logan deal with those things is more interesting and makes him a more formidable villain because, not only does he have to combat people coming at him from below, but also he has to combat them coming from above. It puts the villain in more of a pressure cooker and therefore, makes him more dangerous and interesting."

Research Files

Air Marshal: When Jack sneaks onto the plane, he finds the seat of the air marshal and subdues him for his gun. The Federal Air Marshal Service is a government agency under the Transportation Security Administration branch of the Department of Homeland Security. They are charged with maintaining civil confidence in airline travel and protecting passengers in the case of hostile actions against airports or carriers. The Service was created in 1968 with six volunteers from the FAA that were trained in firearms. The program has since grown and broadened its reach with pilot programs covering buses, light rail, passenger rail systems and ferries. Air marshals are now trained in basic law enforcement, as well as precision marksmanship, which is a mandatory job function due to the tight quarters and pressurization issues with airplanes. All marshals board aircraft first so they can inspect for any potential problems and they are armed with a SIG-Sauer P229 service pistol.

Additional Intel

Fans of Jean Smart's career may recognize that pilot Stan Cotter was played by actor Richard Gilliland, the actresses' real-life husband. The pair met in 1986 when they were working on the show *Designing Women*.

3:00 am - 4:00 am

Director: Brad Turner

Writer: Manny Coto

Guest Cast: Stephen Spinella (Miles Papazian), Paul McCrane (Graem), Jayne Atkinson (Karen Hayes), Julian Sands (Vladimir Bierko), Jude Ciccolella (Mike Novick)

"You know what really gets me, Charles? That you had me going for so long... I had no idea you were such a good liar. If I wasn't so horrified by the fact that I married you, I might be impressed." Martha Logan

Timeframe	Key Events

3:00 A.M. Jack calls Karen and confirms he has the tape.

3:02 A.M. Curtis lets Audrey know Heller survived.

3:04 A.M. Graem tells Logan he can rig a distress call from the plane as an excuse to shoot it down.

3:08 A.M. The distress call is made and Admiral Kirkland advises Logan to shoot the plane down. Logan agrees.

3:10 A.M. Karen calls Jack, who asks for an open freeway to touch down.

3:14 A.M. Chloe is summoned by Karen and Buchanan to help Jack.

3:18 A.M. Jack pushes the co-pilot to land the plane before the F-18 shoots them down.

3:20 A.M. With the dangerous landing, the Admiral recommends they abort, but Logan is adamant they shoot the plane down. He finally relents.

3:21 A.M. The plane smashes onto the freeway.

3:22 A.M. The passengers survive and Jack runs.

3:28 A.M. Jack hides from the Marines and calls Curtis to rendezvous.

3:30 A.M. Miles confronts Karen about working with the "enemies", and she finally tells him the truth.

3:34 A.M. Bierko is transported to a new facility.

3:40 A.M. Logan is stunned that the Marines did not find Jack. Novick is confused by his reaction.

3:43 A.M. At CTU, Jack hands over the recorder to Chloe.

3:44 A.M. Jack and Audrey reunite.

3:45 A.M. Logan calls Graem defeated. He says he will not implicate anyone and opens a box containing a pistol.

3:51 A.M. Logan goes to Martha to apologize. She has nothing but loathing for him.

3:55 A.M. Back in his office with the pistol. Logan gets a call from Miles about Jack.

3:57 A.M. Miles tells Logan of the tape and requests his permission to intervene. Logan is back in the game.

3:59 A.M. Miles surreptitiously flash-erases the evidence tape.

The plane comes in for a landing.

Logan prepares to end it all.

Miles pulls a fast one on Chloe.

While Karen and Miles walked into CTU as allies, they certainly don't end the season that way. Their heated exchange in this episode is a turning point that clearly defines their differing allegiances. Discussing the scene, Jayne Atkinson remembers, "This scene with Stephen Spinella [who plays Miles] is very good! When they come into CTU they are different, but not that different. You see the history of two people who have worked together a long time. She trusts him and she goes with her guts, while he is afraid to. I love the scene because it separates the men from the boys. It also turns out to be very sad for him and her. It is very passionate and Karen is finally coming around to the idea that something is wrong. She

knows she could lose everything if she trusts him. It's a great moment and not many heads of CTU have done that. It's a transformation for Karen. To have somebody who believes in the President and that office and the policies, to challenge them and go against it is painful and hard and sad, but it's right."

Atkinson adds that the producers allowed them to tweak the scene to their liking. "We were doing one of our final scenes and we just wanted a little bit more from it, so we talked to Howard Gordon. He asked us what we wanted to do and we told him and he said it was great. We just took what was there and added our own spin to it because we had been living as those people, which [the producers] value. I've been on shows where you change a word and they get upset. They have such a well-oiled machine here that they trust who they bring on and that is such a gift. I am at a point in my life where, honestly, if you don't have a better idea than me, you need to step away." Smiling, with a twinkle in her eye, Atkinson adds, "I know what I am doing. I've been doing this a *long* time."

Research Files

Hijack Distress Call: Graem tells President Logan that he can rig a distress call from the plane to help convince the military to shoot the plane down. When an airplane, vehicle or ship finds itself in a state of emergency, the operators can signal a distress call to alert others of the situation and a need for immediate help. Distress calls are usually made by radio signal, but they can also be made through sound with loud horns or alarms. Aircraft have their own distress channel called the aircraft emergency frequency. Civilian planes use the 121.5 MHz frequency or the International Air Distress; while military planes utilize the 243.0 MHz frequency called Military Air Distress. The civilian frequency is monitored by air traffic control and emergency services. Recently the Air Line Pilots Association recommended specific counter procedures in the case of suicidal hijackers, including drastic aerial maneuvers to disorient them or depressurizing the cabin.

Additional Intel

Producers created an inadvertent reunion of the cult classic film *RoboCop* in their halls by casting Peter Weller, Ray Wise and Paul McCrane this season. All three actors appeared in the 1987 movie.

4:00 am - 5:00 am

Director: Brad Turner
Writers: David Fury & Sam Montgomery

Guest Cast: Paul McCrane (Graem), Jayne Atkinson (Karen Hayes), Julian Sands (Vladimir Bierko), Peter Weller (Christophe Henderson), Glenn Morshower (Agent Aaron Pierce)

"You're a traitor to this country and a disgrace to your office. And it's my duty to see that you're brought to justice for what you've done. Is there anything else, Charles?" Agent Aaron Pierce

Timeframe — Key Events

4:00 A.M. Chloe checks the tape and there's nothing on it.

4:02 A.M. Jack goes after Miles.

4:03 A.M. Miles says he's been transferred to the White House. Karen slaps him and he leaves.

4:07 A.M. CTU is alerted that Bierko escaped the transfer with another Sentox canister.

4:14 A.M. Logan visits a beaten Pierce in the stables. The Agent berates the President for shaming the Office.

4:17 A.M. Logan calls Graem about the tape, Pierce and his plan to get Jack.

4:19 A.M. Novick tells an upset Logan about Bierko.

4:20 A.M. With no leads, Karen and Buchanan offer a deal to Henderson for information; he agrees.

4:29 A.M. Jack gets fourteen names Henderson says Bierko may contact.

4:31 A.M. Chloe tracks down Victor Malina who Henderson says he can crack. With no choice, Karen orders Jack to go with him.

4:34 A.M. At the stables, Martha sees an agent with a gun. Pierce is fighting for his life when Martha walks in. She surprises the agent and then shoots him.

4:40 A.M. Curtis, Jack and Henderson arrive at Malina's loft.

4:43 A.M. On the roof, Jack hears Henderson rat out CTU. Curtis sends in the team.

4:44 A.M. Curtis is shot, Malina is killed and Jack corners Henderson.

4:46 A.M. Henderson says he was getting files. Jack sends the files to Chloe.

4:52 A.M. Pierce asks Martha to tell Novick the truth.

4:54 A.M. Chloe finds files on a Russian nuclear sub. Jack and Henderson helicopter to it. Jack alerts the navy.

4:58 A.M. Bierko puts a canister into the sub and kills the crew inside.

4:59 A.M. In gas masks, Bierko and his men board and commandeer the weapons system.

Logan confronts a bloodied Pierce.

Bierko is back!

The nuclear sub is armed.

The quiet face-off between a beaten, but undefeated Agent Aaron Pierce and a smug President Logan remains one of actor Glenn Morshower's favorite *24* scenes. "There is a moment in that speech, which for me is my all-time favorite scene in five seasons, between Aaron and Logan. The President walks in and says, 'I'm sorry.' In that scene, I can feel the audience behind me saying, 'Yes!' [Pierce] knows it doesn't matter now so it's clearly safe to speak his mind and he tells the President how he feels about everything and he pulls no punches. Logan then says, 'Are my terms acceptable, Aaron?' Pierce replies, 'With all due respect, Mr. President, there is nothing you have said or done that is acceptable to me in the least. You are

a traitor to this country and a disgrace to this office. And it's my duty to see that you are brought to justice for what you've done.'

"It's an outstanding speech! It's as good as good gets. We both went there and I've never seen a more in-the-moment scene that I've been a part of in any show in thirty-one years. We did one last take and I asked [director] Brad Turner to change a line, it was just one word. I didn't want to tell Brad, I wanted to do it for him and I wanted Greg to react to it too. So I said the line, 'It's my duty to see that you are brought to justice for what you've done. Is there anything else, *Charles*?' I called him 'Charles' and you should have seen the look. Greg pulled back and there were no more words in the scene, and man, he wore the hit of that. Six days later, I went to explain to Howard [Gordon] what I had done. I very seldom change any words but it felt powerful and I wanted them to have it as an option. One of the editors said, 'You mean the 'Charles' moment? It's done.' They walked me to the editing room and showed it to me and I almost cried."

Research Files

Russian Sub: Bierko commandeers a Russian submarine to launch its nuclear warheads on US soil. The Soviet Navy was once considered one of the preeminent sea-based military operations in the world. Their nuclear submarines possessed incredible speed and high-level reactor technology. The Russian Typhoon class sub was also the world's largest. Unfortunately, the Russian nuclear sub fleet was also categorized by its large number of tragic accidents, resulting in many deaths and even a reactor leak on the K-19. Since the end of the Cold War in 1991, the Russian Navy has not been a priority as it once was under the Communist government.

Additional Intel

Glenn Morshower reveals that Agent Pierce was supposed to die this year, shot in the back of the head by one of Logan's men. Heart-broken by that scripted death, Morshower sent an impassioned last minute email appeal to Howard Gordon asking for Pierce to be spared — and it worked.

5:00 am - 6:00 am

Director: Jon Cassar
Writers: Howard Gordon & Evan Katz

Guest Cast: Carlo Rota (Morris O'Brian), Paul McCrane (Graem) Glenn Morshower (Agent Aaron Pierce), Jude Ciccolella (Mike Novick), Tom Wright (Admiral Kirkland)

"Cut him deep and cut him fast." Jack Bauer

Timeframe   Key Events

5:00 A.M. Bierko starts the countdown to bomb a city to punish the Americans.
5:01 A.M. Audrey alerts the navy that the sub is under terrorist control.
5:02 A.M. Jack, Henderson and the TAC team have to stop Bierko themselves.
5:03 A.M. Henderson refuses to board without a weapon.
5:06 A.M. Chloe finds a distress signal from Rooney, a surviving engineer. She coordinates with him to get Jack into the sub.
5:11 A.M. Jack instructs Rooney how to kill a terrorist blocking the entry. The TAC team invades the sub.
5:12 A.M. The sub missile doors open for launch.
5:14 A.M. Rooney causes a distraction. Bierko goes to investigate and Jack kills the lone man in the control room.
5:17 A.M. Henderson works on reversing the launch.
5:19 A.M. Jack has a brutal fight with Bierko, whose neck is snapped. Henderson stops the launch.
5:20 A.M. Henderson disappears. Jack follows and finds him on deck with gun drawn. Henderson pulls the trigger but the gun doesn't contain any bullets. Jack shoots Henderson dead.
5:29 A.M. Jack tells Chloe he is going after Logan and she agrees to help.
5:30 A.M. Logan is relieved Bierko has been stopped. He asks Novick to draft a statement for the press.
5:31 A.M. Martha intercepts Novick. Logan calls Graem about Henderson.
5:32 A.M. Martha and Pierce tell Novick the whole truth and he believes them. He offers to take Pierce off the retreat.
5:41 A.M. Jack calls Novick and Pierce to say he's heading to the retreat to get Logan to confess.
5:43 A.M. Chloe asks for clearance for a new tech – her ex-husband, Morris.
5:46 A.M. Novick asks Martha to detain Logan for Jack.
5:54 A.M. Martha comes to Logan and seduces him to delay his departure.
5:59 A.M. Jack enlists Pierce's help to get on the Presidential helicopter.

Jack breaks Bierko's neck.

Henderson is dead.

Martha seduces Logan.

The final showdown at the Russian nuclear sub was shot on location at the US Navy Facility in San Diego, California. Key assistant for locations, Yoshi Enoki, explains how it took a massive amount of coordination to pack up the entire production and head south. "The initial scout was done through the producers, writers and locations manager, KC Warnke. They asked the US Navy people about the best place to do the submarine scene and San Diego, California ended up being the place." Because of the physical space limitations of the sub, Enoki says it was a rough shoot. "For the crew, getting the equipment into the sub was very tight. There were some scenes where the camera couldn't even pan, because the magazine and the lens

were so far out, it hit the wall. Since our show is all about the handheld look, if you look at the episode there are quite a few scenes where they lock the camera down and you have guys running at the camera or going away. Also, lighting the whole sub to make it look like the rest of the show was hard. We ended up with a small piece of it being built on our stage. It was completely not to scale, but it worked out."

The showdown on the sub also featured the anticipated final face-off between Jack and Henderson. Peter Weller says on separate occasions he and the writers, and then he and Kiefer, worked on the scene tirelessly to get it just right. "We worked out more of a denouement for the death scene. It didn't need to be heroic, but it needed an acknowledgement that this *is* the way the world of guns and power works. We had to come up with something to nail down that this is the game: I kill Tony — Jack kills me now. It's the way of international, real-politick. I'm usually like a dog to make a scene right, and Kiefer appreciated that. But he's like a dog making the scenes right too. I've rarely met an actor on a TV series who is that committed to working a scene into being the best that it can be. I think the scenes between he and I are powerful because we kept carving it into something good. It was very satisfying."

Research Files

Marine One: At the retreat, the Presidential helicopter, known as Marine One, is prepared for the departure of President Logan. One of the preferred modes of transport for the Executive-in-Chief, Marine One is one of nineteen helicopters maintained and operated by the Marines to carry the President. Marine One always flies as part of a pack of choppers, with the others serving as decoys to deter any would-be assassins from centering on one target. As with the Presidential limo, Marine One is taken overseas anytime the President travels as an alternative secure mode of transportation. The helicopter is actually the safest mode of transportation for the President because of the environmental control factors, but operation of the fleet is costly and sometimes logistically challenging, depending on the environment for landing. The first Presidential chopper was created in 1957 for Dwight D. Eisenhower. In the near future the VH-71 Kestrel will become the new model of helicopter for the Marine One fleet.

Additional Intel

The fifth season of *24* was nominated for twelve Emmy awards, including Best Supporting Actor nominations for Greg Itzin and Jean Smart. They were the first actors, aside from Kiefer Sutherland, to ever get nominated for their work on *24*.

6:00 am - 7:00 am

Director: Jon Cassar
Writer: Robert Cochran

Guest Cast: Jude Ciccolella (Mike Novick), Glenn Morshower (Agent Aaron Pierce), Tzi Ma (Cheng Zhi), Carlo Rota (Morris O'Brian), Jayne Atkinson (Karen Hayes)

"You surely must be aware, Mr Bauer, that China has a long memory. Only eighteen months ago, you invaded our territory and killed our Consul. Did you really think that we would forget?" Cheng Zhi

Timeframe

Key Events

6:01 A.M. Jack steals a helicopter flight outfit.

6:07 A.M. Jack commandeers the chopper and agents. He handcuffs a stunned Logan.

6:11 A.M. They land and Jack forces Logan into a warehouse, empties his pockets and handcuffs him to a pole.

6:13 A.M. Morris arrives and hands a briefcase to Jack.

6:14 A.M. Jack calls Chloe — they have ten minutes.

6:18 A.M. Jack sets up a webcam connected to Chloe and demands a confession.

6:22 A.M. Jack raises his gun to Logan, but he can't shoot.

6:23 A.M. A TAC team invades. Jack gives up. Chloe types and then shuts down the feed.

6:24 A.M. Logan retrieves his belongings and tells the guards that Jack is delusional.

6:29 A.M. Novick tells Martha that Jack failed.

6:30 A.M. As Palmer's hearse arrives Martha accuses Logan of being a murderer.

6:32 A.M. Logan grabs Martha and smacks her around. He threatens to have her committed.

6:39 A.M. Logan and Martha rejoin the podium.

6:40 A.M. Chloe reveals Jack planted a listening device on Logan and she recorded his confession to Martha. Chloe calls the Attorney General.

6:45 A.M. After eulogizing Palmer, the Secret Service swarm Logan and his confession is revealed.

6:46 A.M. A shocked Logan is led away.

6:47 A.M. Jack and Audrey reunite. A call from Kim takes Jack away.

6:48 A.M. There is no call and Jack is chloroformed by masked men and kidnapped.

6:53 A.M. Karen apologizes to Buchanan and assures him that he will not be fired.

6:57 A.M. Beaten and bloody, Jack is taken to Cheng.

6:59 A.M. Jack is put on a boat to China.

Logan gets a reprieve.

Palmer is laid to rest.

Jack's on his way to China!

After the villains are stopped and the world is safe again, Jack and Audrey get a rare, albeit fleeting moment to reunite once more. "I'm a romantic and as I'm playing Audrey, she wants them to be together more than anything," Kim Raver says about the pair. "Hopefully, what makes the drama is that yearning of finally being together and it being ripped out from under her. I think it also goes back to the emotional core that people root for Audrey and Jack. I want them to be together and I'm aware the show is always somewhat tragic, but that hope keeps people wanting their relationship to continue. You never know what's going to happen on *24*." Famous last words for sure as Jack is kidnapped by the Chinese in the last seconds of the

episode to forcibly repay his outstanding debt to them.

Tzi Ma, who plays head of security for the Chinese Consulate, Cheng Zhi, says his call to return for the season five finale was an utter surprise. "It was absolutely unexpected, but time doesn't stand still. A little insight for the fans is that they watch the season but a lot of time elapses from the end of the previous season. In the off-season, it's almost like a new sport because during the off-season people are out doing other stuff — like me. But [the producers] had been anticipating the next season like spring training. Yet for me, it was totally unexpected. It was really fun because it really raised the stakes. I thought the way they shot it was brilliant. You didn't really know where the hell Jack was! You just know he is hurt and it's dark and it's big — that placed echoed! It was a great cliffhanger. You have to hand it to these writers. They have such an insight into suspense. I don't know what they do when they go home, maybe they pop out on their wives," he laughs.

Research Files

Presidential Funeral: President David Palmer is finally laid to rest during a state funeral. In the United States, state funerals are legally mandated for sitting Presidents, a President-elect, and any former Presidents. While state funerals are formal events, there are no specific guidelines for the process as the early forefathers did not wish to emulate the established practices of the British Empire. It wasn't until the assassination of Abraham Lincoln that the country observed its first national mourning period, with the President laid out in the US Capitol rotunda. Today, all Presidents are required to draw up their funeral plans once they are sworn into office. In total, eleven Presidents have been honored with state viewings and national days of mourning. While all funerals have been different, there are some elements present in each, including a twenty-one-gun salute, a caisson pulled by six horses and a flag draped over the coffin.

Additional Intel

Actor Carlo Rota, who plays Chloe's ex-husband Morris O'Brian, is a renowned foodie and host of the hit Canadian culinary series, *The Great Canadian Food Show*.

Writing 24

An in-depth look into the writing of
episodes 5:00 pm – 6:00 pm
and 6:00 pm – 7:00 pm

Any writer for scripted television will tell you that coming up with the ideas, story arcs, plot points and character motivations for the twenty-two episodes needed to make up a one-hour drama's season is an exhausting, complicated, but (eventually) rewarding experience. On 24 there's also the bonus of coming up with two more episodes a year than the average show, tempered by the restrictions of writing within a real-time format. There are no time cuts or flashbacks used to advance the story; it's the here and the now and that's it. 24 is also a thriller that balances upwards of five to six interweaving storylines per episode at a breakneck pace that eats up plot in an astonishingly short span of episodes. What all of that means is that every episode of 24 gets a lot of rewrites before audiences get to see the final product, which took weeks to whittle down to forty-three minutes of exhilarating television.

Every episode goes through an arduous story-breaking process where the writers plot out the beats (or important moments) of the episode. After the beats are determined, the writer of the episode creates the outline, which then gets reviewed and revised. After that, the first draft is written based on the latest changes, which is then turned in and often rewritten again from scratch.

No two episodes in a season come together exactly the same way, as evidenced by the production stories for the important season five, mid-season episodes, '5:00 pm – 6:00 pm' (episode eleven) and '6:00 pm – 7:00 pm' (episode twelve). Considered the halfway point of the 24 season, traditionally these episodes contain important milestones where major changes, or twists, emerge to help propel the season towards its eventual finale. Because of their importance, a lot of extra work goes into making sure they point the story in the right direction. Story editors Matt Michnovetz, Duppy Demetrius and script coordinator Nicole Ranadive were responsible for writing episodes eleven and twelve. Shedding some light on the 24 writing process, Ranadive and Michnovetz dissect how dramatically a script evolves from outline to final product.

5.00 pm – 6.00 pm

A 24 script coordinator for two seasons, Nicole Ranadive's first script written for broadcast television was episode eleven (see page fifty-two for script summary). Ranadive explains how the writers at 24 start a script: "Generally, a story is broken, it's written and then nine times out of ten, they re-break it. I think most shows take care to make really detailed outlines and go through the process of the outline, so by the time you go to write it, it's almost there. With this show, outlines are more like beat sheets and are not detailed. So a lot of the time, it will look like it works on the outline but once you get it in a draft form, you realize the elements that don't work and so it's re-broken. From the very first writer's draft to the second writer's draft, there is usually a lot of change."

Each draft of a script is color-coded, so the edit stages are clear for the writers and the production crew. On 24, the first draft is white, and then the colors follow: blue, pink, yellow, green, gold and then it goes back to second white. "I don't think we've had any script not go into second colors," Ranadive smiles. "Next we have a concept meeting and there are always changes after that because of production issues. Then the writers will go in and fine-tune it again. After that, we have the production meeting with locations and those changes will go into the script because of what locations we scouted. And then there is a producer's read-through, and there is always another full draft after that for tinkering and dialogue changes. The producers' meeting is done the day before we start shooting, but there are always changes into production. Every once in a while, the actors may have some thoughts about a script so they'll talk to Howard [Gordon] about changes for a scene that might shoot the next day.

"I remember that episode ten [4pm – 5pm], which Evan Katz wrote, was changing a lot and consequently that kept changing episode eleven. I had broken it with Manny and Joel, so I went home to write it. I had about a week to write my script, but, literally halfway through, I was getting calls about changes. Once I turned in the first draft they said,

'This is great but... we have a different idea. This doesn't work so we are going to pull it apart and put it back together."

Explaining where the story was at the time, Ranadive reveals that one of many changes was, "We were not going to shoot Miriam Henderson in the knee," Ranadive explains about the scene where Jack holds the Hendersons at gunpoint in their home. "Initially, it was just going to be a threat because the question was, would Jack Bauer do that? I think after a couple of drafts we realized, yeah, maybe Jack would do it! He's been pushed to that point and enough lives were at stake. It was a big moment and a big decision."

The following are script excerpts from the original scene and the final on-air scene:

          JACK
          Where's the nerve gas?

          CHRIS
          I don't know!

Jack FIRES again. The bullet strikes closer this time, SHATTERING a
chunk of the coffee table a couple of feet away from Miriam.

          MIRIAM
          Stop it... Stop it...

Jack aims again.

          CHRIS
          No!

Chris lunges for Jack. Jack backhands him with his pistol, CRACKING
him aside the face and sending him reeling against the wall. Jack
moves to Chris.

          JACK
          I'll do it, Chris. I'll kill her.

          CHRIS
          Jack, I'm begging you to stop this.

          JACK
          The terrorists are threatening to set off nineteen canisters
          of nerve gas! That's hundreds of thousands of people!

Jack spins and FIRES again. This time, the SLUG tears into the couch
just inches from Miriam's head. Miriam SCREAMS again. But Jack isn't
finished. He strides over to Miriam and stands over her. This time,
the pistol is aimed directly at the back of Miriam's head. Miriam's
on the floor, sobbing hysterically. Chris, blood streaming down the
side of his face from where Jack pistol-whipped him, is wrenched by
the sight of his wife like this.

          JACK (CONT'D)
          I will pull this trigger, but it won't be me who's killing
          her...

Jack chambers another round.

          JACK (CONT'D)
          I'm sorry, Miriam...

Jack's finger tightens around the trigger.

          CHRIS
          Jack... don't... don't...

Jack looks at Chris. A seemingly endless moment. And then Jack draws
the gun away. Jack and Chris trade a look. For a split second,
Chris' eyes flash victory. Then Jack kneels down beside Miriam,
looks her in the eye.

JACK
He was ready to let you die, Miriam.

Miriam sits up, looks at her husband, seeing him in a vastly different light.

SHOOTING DRAFT
INT. HENDERSON'S HOUSE

MIRIAM (CONT'D)
Then it's true, what Jack's been saying...

But Christopher's continuing silence confirms his guilt.

MIRIAM (CONT'D)
You've been lying to me this whole time.

CHRISTOPHER
I swear I was only trying to protect you.

MIRIAM
By lying to me?

CHRISTOPHER
It's not that simple.

MIRIAM
I defended you.

CHRISTOPHER
And I defended you. From things you didn't need to know. Because I love you. That's the truth, Miriam. That's always been the truth. You know that. I know you do.

Which Miriam finds herself unable to refute. After a beat, Christopher reaches toward Miriam, cradles her face gently. She allows his comfort, rests her face against his hand in a gesture of forgiveness.

CHRISTOPHER (CONT'D)
Whatever I did... it was never out of self-interest or greed. Even after they took me out of service, I still served this country.

Their tender moment suddenly interrupted when Jack FIRES a bullet into Miriam, just above her kneecap. Miriam SCREAMS as she goes down, clutching her leg.

CHRISTOPHER (CONT'D)
Son of a bitch, what the hell are you doing?!

Jack regards Christopher, point-blank:

JACK
I didn't hit her kneecap, Chris. She'll still be able to walk, but if I have to shoot her again, she will be in a wheelchair for the rest of her life.

Jack presses his gun against Miriam's kneecap.

Detailing another change, Ranadive says, "At the end of episode ten, Jack was at Omicron getting sabotaged by Henderson with a bomb, and the motorcade was getting blown up. I believe the motorcade was going to be in eleven, but they moved it to the end of episode ten, so the top of episode eleven was now the aftermath. Kim Bauer was going to be brought back in episode eleven, but she got pushed to episode twelve."

In the final script, Curtis Manning is able to find and remove an armed Sentox gas canister before it's unleashed in a hospital. Ranadive continues, "It was going to be a fake bomb with a phony canister that was a distraction for a different target. But we went through several drafts of that and realized that it didn't work. It was decided that the bomb needed to be a real threat,

and so once we decided it was a real bomb we had to make a hero moment for Curtis."

Another huge shift in episode eleven is exactly how Tony Almeida dies. "All of the Tony material had been lifted from a previous episode, because he was going to show up in an earlier episode but they pushed his reappearance until eleven," Ranadive details. "In the original draft, Tony was going to kill Henderson at Henderson's house. He was going to find out that Henderson was responsible for Michelle's death, bust out of CTU and find Henderson's house. Tony was going to see that Jack was working with Henderson and then kill Henderson. Then it changed so that Jack was going to kill Tony to save Henderson because he needed Henderson."

6:00 pm – 7:00 pm

Matt Michnovetz immediately followed through on the action in episode twelve (see page fifty-six for script summary). "The producers and creators were split. A couple of them were away and a couple of them were here, so they hadn't exactly agreed on all the beats. The beat sheet hadn't been completely approved by everybody so there were dissenting opinions still floating around, which meant it was constantly changing. I wrote it with Duppy Demetrius, my writing partner in season five, and we started and immediately ran into some problems, so we started re-breaking it. We had a week to write it, which is a fair amount of time, but we spent a week trying to get the beat sheet down. We were going down the hall, knocking on the door going, 'Sorry to bother you, but we've got a couple of questions...' The original story, which is based on the loose ending of Tony being dead, starts off with Jack over Tony's body and Henderson sitting there glaring at him. Henderson basically says to Jack that he has an assassin who has Kim Bauer in his crosshairs. If the guy doesn't hear from him, Henderson will have him pull the trigger.

"The idea was that she was going to be in a house with this older man that she had married, who eventually became the Barry Landes character," Michnovetz continues. "We had written him a little different than how C. Thomas Howell portrayed him. He was a little weirder, but you could still see how she was comforted by him. Meanwhile, there was a sniper or a bomb expert perched nearby. We got into this whole thing of how Jack would bring Henderson into CTU and then take out this guy. Then we thought maybe a second team with Curtis would take the guy out. We started writing and then everything changed. It was then decided to have Henderson's sniper in CTU's interrogation room two, and Henderson in interrogation room one. Kim was going to be brought into CTU, instead of voluntarily coming down with Barry. She was going to be asked to come down by agents and then thrown into another holding room.

"We also had a bunch of little scenes between Audrey and Kim, and one of them stayed into the final script. Audrey is showing Kim the ropes on how she dealt with finding out that the man she loved had returned. We also had a lot more creepy scenes with Kim's psychiatrist playing with her head and being really manipulative."

The following are script excerpts from the original scene and the final on-air scene:

ORIGINAL SCENE
INT. CTU - CONFERENCE ROOM

Kim enters, turns to Audrey as she closes the door.

> KIM
> So what am I doing here?

> AUDREY
> This is awkward for me, Kim... and it's going to be hard for you to
> hear.

> KIM
> Whatever it is, just tell me.

Audrey chooses her words carefully, then:

> AUDREY
> It's about your father...

> KIM
> My father's dead.

> AUDREY
> No, Kim, he's not.

Kim blinks, not sure she's heard Audrey right.

> AUDREY (CONT'D)
> I didn't know myself until a few hours ago. But he's alive.

> KIM
> That's impossible. I was at his funeral. We both were.

> AUDREY
> It wasn't his body we buried that day.

Kim's knees buckle under the weight of this. She lowers herself into a chair.

> AUDREY (CONT'D)
> It's complicated... Your father found out someone inside the govern-
> ment wanted him dead. He had no choice.

> KIM
> So he played dead...?

> AUDREY
> Something like that.

> KIM
> But he couldn't tell me.

> AUDREY
> He thought you might be in danger. He didn't want to expose you.

> KIM
> Where is he?

> AUDREY
> He'll be here soon.

Kim nods, but doesn't know what to do with this. The two of them stand in
silence for a moment.

> KIM
> I need some time. Alone.

> AUDREY
> I understand.

NEW SCENE
INT. CTU - FIELD OPS OFFICE

Audrey's expecting a warmer greeting, but Kim is guarded.

                KIM
                Hi. This is Barry Landes.

                AUDREY
                (shakes his hand)
                Audrey Raines.

                KIM
                So what is it? What did you need to talk to me about that's so impor-
                tant?

                AUDREY
                Actually, I think it would be better to talk about this in private.

        Which Audrey says with a polite smile to Barry.

                KIM
                Whatever you have to say to me you can say in front of Barry.

                AUDREY
                Kim, I really...

                BARRY
                You heard her, Ms. Raines.

Audrey takes a beat, would very much like not to do this in front of Barry,
but realizes she has no choice.

                AUDREY
                This is awkward for me, Kim... I'm not sure how to start...

                KIM
                Then just say it.

Audrey chooses her words carefully.

                AUDREY
                It's about your father...

                KIM
                What about him?

                AUDREY
                He's alive.

                KIM
                You're lying.

                BARRY
                What kind of sick joke is this?

Audrey's silence tells Kim this isn't a joke at all. Kim shakes her head, and
backs away... until she's next to Barry. She reaches for his hand.

                AUDREY
                It's the truth, but it's complicated... there's an explanation.
                (off Kim's still stunned silence)
                Someone inside the government wanted your father dead. If he'd just
                run away, he knew they'd come after you. He knew you wouldn't be safe
                as long as he was alive. So he staged his own death and went under-
                ground. He couldn't tell you because he was afraid it would put you
                in danger. I didn't know myself until this morning...

Kim is overwhelmed, doesn't know what to do with what she's just been told.

Michnovetz recalls another element of the episode that went through several versions: "We also had this recurring story with this key card being stolen and evil Ostroff taking the canister into CTU, which got changed around a lot. First, we had the files that Chloe was decrypting; they are put on hold because of the nerve gas that goes off in CTU. They don't get through them until episode fourteen [8pm – 9pm], where they get the name of Collette Stenger. Usually we compact things, but we dragged that out. In this draft, they actually find the name."

Michnovetz also reveals that his version featured even more death than what ended up onscreen. "When Duppy and I sat down with Joel and Bob and Michael Loceff, they said they were going to repopulate CTU — which is the Homeland story. So we were killing everybody!" he laughs. "The season started with everyone dying, so we thought it would be a continuation of the madness if halfway through, you just kill off everyone else, except for Chloe. It turned out that poor Edgar was the only one to die."

One of the most unlikely stories considered was an extension to the Logan family tree. "Logan also had a crazy brother that showed up at the house and was hitting on Martha," Michnovetz chuckles. "Martha/Pierce actually came out of Martha and Logan's brother. That turned into Martha and Pierce in *A Remains of the Day* type of story."

The following is an extract from an unused scene between Martha and Logan:

Logan sees the dining room is set.

LOGAN
Who's coming?

MARTHA
Your brother.

LOGAN
I don't want to see my brother!

MARTHA
It's just for one night and your brother's own safety.

"The next beat was that Logan tells Novick that he hates his brother," Michnovetz continues. "He's a rich yachtsman and a widower. Logan is then called away to deal with the CTU crisis and when he returns he sees Martha and his brother laughing, having a little too good of a time.

"We finally ended up finishing the script in a weekend," Michnovetz says. "But they changed it again and we did a new beat sheet. We got a little bit of a pass on the second one and we kept pushing it. We had so many people come in and get involved — it went through at least second white or blue. But they turned out to be pretty solid episodes. I'm a fan of the show too and I'm really happy with them."

In Memoriam: David Palmer

Career:

Former President of the United States
United States Congress, Senator (MD)
Senate Appropriations Committee – Member
Senate Commerce Subcommittee – Member
United States Congress, Representative (MD)
House Ethics Committee – Chairman
House Ways and Means Committee – Member
House National Security Subcommittee – Member
Maryland State Congress, Representative (Baltimore)
Fidley, Barrow & Bain, Attorney at Law

Expertise:

Foreign Diplomacy

Personal:

Spouse (divorced) – Sherry Palmer (deceased)
Son – Keith Palmer
Daughter – Nicole Palmer
Brother – Wayne Palmer
Sister – Sandra Palmer

Death:

Assassinated at approximately 7:02 am, Los Angeles, California

David Palmer R.I.P.

From a frontrunner candidate to a retired President, David Palmer was a politician that transcended party affiliation to become a model for what any person in elected office could aspire to. Honorable, wise and a true statesman, Palmer weathered many storms over the span of almost a decade in public service. Together with Jack Bauer, the two men helped stave the country from the brink of war and nuclear attack. Behind closed doors, Palmer dealt with personal disappointment and betrayal, delivered by the hands of his ex-wife, Sherry Palmer. Yet he held such high regard for his role as Commander-in-Chief that he tried desperately to preserve the integrity of his administration despite the Machiavellian machinations of his former wife. When he could no longer maintain that balance without tainting the Presidency with the fallout of her improprieties, Palmer chose not to seek a second term. His upstanding belief in the country and the way it should be run was an unparalleled example of leadership in action.

The Cast Reflects:

Actor DB Woodside was introduced in the third season as David's more impulsive younger brother, Wayne Palmer. Together they labored through the intrigues that threatened to bring down David's Presidency, while off-screen, the actors were just as close. Woodside says of Haysbert, "Dennis was just amazing to me. I can't speak highly enough of that guy. He brought me in and was so nice to me. He was everything that a new actor on a show wants. When you are coming onto an established show, it can be a nightmare or a fear and Dennis made me feel so welcomed. He is one of the best storytellers I know, as well as being one of the most articulate men that I know. I love to hear his spin on politics and the inner workings of the business. He alone has taught me so much. He is just a good guy and a good friend. Even in season six there were a few times I called Dennis for advice, which he gave and helped me so much."

Another close friend to Haysbert is actor Glenn Morshower. It was his character Agent Aaron Pierce's duty to protect the President, but that close bond also translated to real life. "I was originally hired for two episodes," Morshower relates. "What happened was that Dennis and I really liked each other as people and the more [the writers] saw that, the more they wrote it for Palmer and Pierce. We are actually good friends, which made it work on every level. There was no pretending that we adore each other. We *are* brothers. He was with me when my dad died. We've just supported one another through a number of different events."

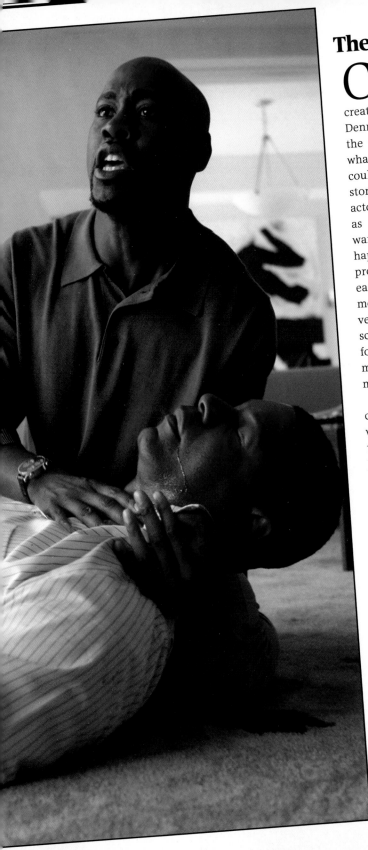

The Producers Reflect:

Co-creator and executive producer Howard Gordon says that David Palmer will always remain one of the most beloved characters created on *24*. Through the fine work done by Dennis Haysbert, David Palmer always surpassed the writers' and the audiences' expectations for what a character committed to serving his country could achieve. "You get a certain confidence that a story is being so beautifully inhabited by these actors that you feel very safe. It draws your interest as a writer and schematically you feel that you want to know more as a writer about what's happening, so you write to these characters. The process with Dennis has always just been a little easier. Part of the reason is that maybe his part was more clearly written. That story always felt very, very clear to us. Every time Dennis has been on screen, we haven't had to vamp or fill out scenes for the sake of filling them. This role was extremely meaningful to him. Dennis took that role, as a role model, very seriously."

Talking about the evolution of Palmer, co-creator Robert Cochran says, "In the first season, we wanted the target of the assassination attempt to be someone you cared about. On one hand, Jack's family is threatened and on the other, he's got to save Palmer's life. If Palmer was a jerk, then there's not much tension. But if you have a guy who you really feel is a good man and a good President and somebody the country needs, then at least it provides a counterbalance to the personal pressures for Jack, because he genuinely *wants* to save this guy's life. So there was certainly a desire in the first season to make Palmer as appealing as possible. Dennis, as an actor, just nailed it. He came across with such integrity, and such moral courage, without arrogance. So many people have said it and I felt it too: I would love to have this guy *be* President. You didn't even know what his politics were; it was just a question of his character. We loved Dennis as a character and an actor. We started out writing a good candidate and then Dennis just ran with it. After that, we felt we knew who we were writing. We did compromise him over the years, but not in any way that was evil. I think we compromised him in ways that were forced upon him by the nature of politics, living a public life and having a screwed-up family."

In Memoriam: Michelle Dessler

Career:
President, private security company
CTU – Acting Special Agent in Charge, Los Angeles Domestic Unit
CTU – Associate Special Agent in Charge, Division
CTU – Intelligence Agent, Los Angeles Domestic Unit
CTU – Internet Protocol Manager, Los Angeles Domestic Unit
DARPA – High Confidence Systems Working Group, National Institute of Standards & Technology

Expertise:
Built IPSec architecture.
Attacks scripts, computer vulnerabilities, intrusion detection, penetration testing, operational security, viruses
Proficiency in Cerberus and PlutoPlus

Personal:
Spouse: Tony Almeida
Brother: Danny Dessler

Death:
Car bomb explosion at approximately 7:13 am, outside the Almeida/Dessler residence, Southern California

Michelle Dessler R.I.P.

Rising up the ranks of CTU from a Protocol Manager to Acting Special Agent in Charge, Michelle Dessler was a shining example of impressive strength, intelligence and loyalty. She took great pride in her service to her country, and through her heroic work at CTU, where she worked side-by-side with operatives like Jack Bauer, Tony Almeida and Bill Buchanan, she helped bring down terrorist cells bent on unleashing mass destruction on US soil.

A computer security expert, Dessler's keen knowledge and research skills were integral in stopping several extreme enemies of the state, including Marie Warner, Stephen Saunders, and Habib Marwan. Yet arguably, Dessler's finest performance on the job was her handling of the Chandler Hotel virus outbreak. When a deadly pneumatic virus was intentionally released in the hotel, Dessler remained on-site (despite her own potential mortality) and helped contain the plague from reaching outside the quarantine facility.

A rare person willing to sacrifice what was most important to her for the greater good (including the safety of her own spouse during a dire stand-off with the operative known as Mandy), Dessler showed great humanity and dignity in the face of danger. Her sense of duty ultimately led to her demise when the assassination of former President David Palmer compelled her to return to CTU to help track down his killer. Tragically, her efforts were thwarted when she became the victim of a vicious car bomb that killed her and wounded her husband.

Reiko Aylesworth Reflects:

Having spent three full seasons developing Michelle Dessler into a fully realized and achingly human character, Reiko Aylesworth says there was no discontent when it was finally time for Michelle to be sacrificed in the opening of season five. "24 has to be sacrificed in the opening of season five. "24 has a very comic book [style] to it, with male heroes, damsels in distress or 'evil' women," she reflects. "I was very fortunate to play a character that was able to have heart and integrity, but was also competent. I think that gave [Michelle] longevity."

One of the few truly stalwart and honorable characters on 24 that didn't shift allegiances, Dessler was more than just a female role model. She held her own with Jack Bauer and the rest of the government suits, yet her relationship with Tony provided a look at the vulnerable woman with a heart that loved deeply. Aylesworth reveals that she looked to her own family for inspiration in crafting Michelle. "I modeled the character a lot on my mother, who ran a jail. She never tried to grandstand and she is a strong female role model. I wasn't trying to be a male character. I wasn't trying to make a political stand, but at the same time, they gave me this character that is in this position and is very capable, so it was important she held her own with the men. It is a very testosterone-driven show, but I don't think you have to sacrifice the female characters to maintain that."

The loss of Michelle Dessler was a huge blow to fans who had become particularly attached to her over three seasons. For Aylesworth, the legacy of playing Dessler is one she cherishes to this day and she hopes that fans will always remember her character fondly. "I really hope most of all that [fans] remember my character's heart and integrity. I know that Carlos Bernard and I always aimed at having these characters be a way to access these stories into their own lives. You'll never really know what it's like to go out and save the world, but you know what it's like when the person you love most in the world is in danger. A lot of what Carlos and I developed was really just through looks — and the show really allowed that. Because of the context of the twenty-four hours, we couldn't get wrapped up in the romance, so instead you had to pull someone into a corner and say, 'Look, I love

you. If I don't make it today, I just want you to know that I would kill or die for you... okay? Let's go!' I hope that's what people got. It's what I tried to do with Michelle, by showing less of the superhero and more of the human being with all the frailties and mistakes that she made."

The Producers Reflect:

Executive producer Howard Gordon says of Reiko Aylesworth's time on the series: "She fit in so instantly on the show. From a character that didn't have much description in the way of who she was or where she came from, Reiko created that character. She projects an intensity and intelligence. We ended up writing to it, and then seeing the mundane interactions and the chemistry between her and Carlos, all of which showed they looked pretty good together as a couple. That suggested itself pretty quickly to us as a relationship. Obviously, the stuff that we compel these characters to face is not always an easy thing to do and not many people can do it, yet she did it extremely well. We were also very aware of how strong a character she was and we were well aware of preserving that part of her character."

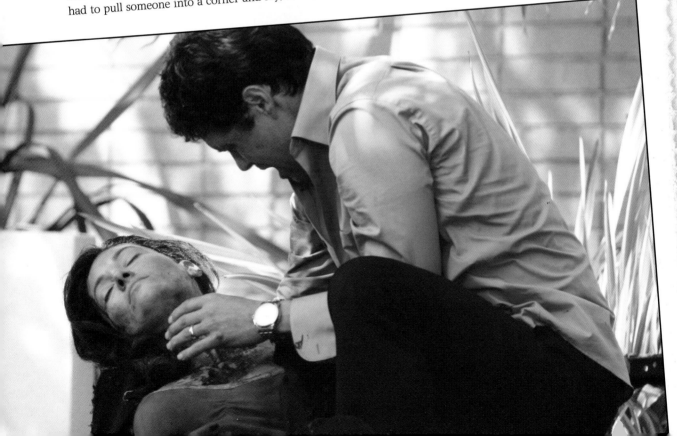

In Memoriam: Walt Cummings

Career:
White House Chief of Staff, President Charles Logan Administration
White House Security Director, President John Keeler and then Acting President Charles Logan

Experience:
Domestic and foreign policy, security tactics and strategy

Personal:
Spouse: Suzanne Cummings

Death:
Murder, faked to look like a suicide at approximately 1:55 pm, The Western White House Retreat, Hidden Valley, California

Walt Cummings R.I.P.

Walt Cummings was a savvy advisor in the White House who quickly established that he was not a fan of Jack Bauer. When the crisis at the Chinese Consulate reached a fever pitch after the friendly fire death of the Chinese Consul, Cummings took it upon himself to order the Secret Service to kill Bauer once he was back in US custody. It was in fact his actions and Charles Logan's lack of support in counteracting Cummings' order that propelled Jack to fake his own death to thwart both Chinese and US death sentences against him. More than a year and a half later, in President Logan's administration, Cummings is revealed to be a mole for a Russian separatist faction responsible for the deaths of former President David Palmer and Michelle Dessler. Cummings attempts to pin the murders on Bauer, but he fails twice, which leads to Bauer seeking him out. After a violent confrontation, Cummings is forced by Bauer to reveal his treasonous behavior. Soon after Cummings is found dead, hanging from the end of a rafter in the retreat by his own tie.

The Producers Reflect:

Walt Cummings, played by John Allen Nelson, became a favorite minor villain for the producers of *24*. Established as a major foe of Jack Bauer's within the White House at the end of season four, Cummings became a logical adversary to follow through into season five. Co-executive producer David Fury explains, "We knew there was going to be a character we called Rasputin, a Rasputin in the White House. We didn't know it was going to be Walt Cummings, although he was the perfect choice because he tried to have Jack killed in season four." Executive producer Howard Gordon continues, "Originally [Rasputin] was another character entirely, but somebody in the writers' room said, 'Why not make it the guy who basically ordered Jack's death a year before? He worked for Logan, so why not let it be him?' There was one little glitch we had in terms of the logic, but it was a pretty small one. We were impressed by the level of John's performance. We thought he was terrific!"

As to Cummings' untimely death, Gordon explains it came out of a couple of factors. "One is that we needed to tie up the corrupt White House strand. He was in some ways the sacrificial lamb. We didn't entirely know at that point that Logan was bad, but the story took us there. [Cummings' death] wasn't something we knew at the beginning of the season, but the story just drove to that point. As much as we loved him, it was time for his character to end."

In Memoriam:
Edgar Stiles

Career:
CTU – Senior Internet protocol manager, Los Angeles
Domestic Unit
CTU – Intelligence Analyst, Los Angeles Domestic Unit
CTU – Internet Protocol Manager, Los Angeles Domestic
Unit

Expertise:
Operating systems, distributed systems, informational
retrieval and wireless networks.

Personal:
Single
Mother – Lucy Stiles (deceased)

Death:
Sentox gas poisoning at approximately 6:59 pm,
Headquarters of CTU, Los Angeles Division

Edgar Stiles R.I.P.

With his soft-spoken voice and his stereotypical, computer hacker shape, CTU Senior Internet Protocol Manager Edgar Stiles never overwhelmed a room like Jack Bauer or managed to throw out a zinger like Chloe O'Brian, but he made an incredible impression none-the-less. A genius on the computer, Stiles proved that desk jockeys can be heroes too when he was able to configure the Dobson Override to stop nearly twenty nuclear plants from melting down and killing millions. Sadly, the only one he couldn't stop was the one closest to his beloved mother, and her life was lost.

Louis Lombardi Reflects:

As a successful character actor known for his colorful parts in shows like *The Sopranos*, Louis Lombardi says taking the role of the tragic cubicle nerd, Edgar Stiles, proved to be the biggest surprise of his entire career. "Conveniently, when I got on the show they had a whole new cast. They gave rebirth to the show with us — all the new actors. It was like a fresh start for me. When I went on the show, I was supposed to be there for no more than two episodes. Immediately after the second show, they kept writing for me. I always have the attitude that things are organic. Things will happen and it will work out, and that's exactly how it happened." Remaining for the entire season, Lombardi says his role just got better and better. "This was the best real acting role I've ever had. It wasn't about being in every scene, but about what you are saying and what you are doing. Never mind my death stuff, but go back to season four with my mother dying and finding out that Marianne [Aisha Tyler] is a spy! Season five was great, but season four was even better for me."

Over his two seasons on the show, Edgar Stiles became one of the most beloved characters on the series — ever. Portly, browbeaten by Chloe O'Brian, and at times a bit of an office tattler, Edgar was hardly the kind of character on paper that looks like a winner, but audiences couldn't get enough of him. "I really realized when it started airing just how much people loved the guy," Lombardi says, still in awe. "The show is almost robotic and that's not a bad thing. Jack

Bauer, Curtis Manning and the people in CTU — they have a job to do no matter what. But when it comes down to Edgar, everyone has an Edgar in their life — a brother, cousin, uncle or father. I think people related to him because he was so human. The reason I know this is because the majority of the fans that still stop me say, 'Oh my God! They call *me* Edgar!' I said to my mom, 'Wow that's pretty amazing. Not everybody knows a Jack Bauer, right or wrong. But *everyone* knows an Edgar.'

"I think what really made audiences love him was the interaction between him and Chloe," Lombardi continues. "It wasn't just Edgar. He was loved, but he was loved for the things he did, like the little things he did with Chloe every episode. It's a team effort. Edgar is really all about Edgar and Chloe combined. People loved their dynamic and the snippets when she called him an idiot." Speaking about his onscreen rapport with Rajskub, Lombardi gushes, "It was easy. It was like working with someone that I had known forever. As soon as they put me in a room with her, I felt like I had known that girl for twenty years. She's adorable and fun."

Lombardi is still genuinely humbled and appreciative of the opportunity to play Edgar until his tragic end. "They killed a human character and that was what was so strong. [To this day] I can't go anywhere, and I'm not exaggerating, whether it's a supermarket, an audition or New York City, fifty-percent of the room knows me as Edgar. No matter what I do, I see this role as being one of my best ever. I could win an Oscar and I will still put this role up there as one of the best roles I've ever had."

The Producers Reflect:

The 24 writers admit they only truly understood the depth of fan love for Edgar Stiles when they wrote his death. Executive producer Howard Gordon remembers, "His relationship with Chloe was particularly sweet. He had this unrequited love for her, which we never hit too hard on the head but I think it was always there. These were two misfits who related and were so good at what they did and I think that's what makes this show so great. Then to sacrifice this loveable character, in that moment, I think we renewed our contract with the audience, proving that everyone is expendable and anything is possible. We brought ourselves pretty close to the edge and we were not unaware that we were taking a big chance. We didn't expect the response — it was stunning. I knew that it would be effective and I knew that he was a loved character, I just didn't know how deeply loved he was. I think part of that is the function of the actor and the way it was shot. It was a very sad moment."

In Memoriam:
Lynn McGill

Career:
CTU Supervisor, Division LA
Acting Special Agent in Charge, CTU LA

Personal:
Sister – Jenny McGill (deceased)

Death:
Sentox gas poisoning at approximately 7:43 pm,
CTU Headquarters, Los Angeles Division

Sean Astin Reflects:

With a career spanning thirty years, including his career-defining role as Samwise the Hobbit in *The Lord of the Rings* trilogy, actor Sean Astin reveals that it was a chance meeting with *24* co-creator Joel Surnow at their chiropractor that scored him the role of Lynn McGill. "Joel asked me about a quarter second after having met me if I wanted to be on the show and I just quickly responded, 'Yes!' I didn't have to think about it.

"I was prepared for it to be a four or five episode arc," Astin reveals about his initial commitment to the show. "I didn't know if I would come in and then just leave. But at the same time, every time you get a new script a little electricity goes through you when you read that you survived at the end. So I didn't ask any questions. I just waited to see what came through and tried to do it to the best of my ability. By the second or third episode it became clear to me what my function in the story was: that I would become the foil for the other characters. It felt totally appropriate for me and it was a good thing for the show. For my part, it was an easy transition from not being on the show to being the character. It was almost silly how easy it was. I nearly questioned if it was working because I just knew how to do it. The character was written in such a way, and I came at it in such a way, that it just fit right from the beginning."

While Lynn McGill seemed to quickly devolve into a chasm of paranoia, Astin says he liked his character and understood his conflict. "The thing I love about him is that he's sort of nice and affable on the one hand and wants to be a good guy, and then he's sort of a complete megalomaniac on the other hand. Just getting to play with those variations is fun to do. A lot of the people I've talked to in Homeland Security, who deal with these issues for real on a daily basis, they have a sense of quiet resolve and calm confidence about what they're doing. The more I learned about Lynn, the more I realized how quickly that can be undermined and just when things go wrong, how it can throw your entire frame of consciousness. It was fun and a really good opportunity."

The Producers Reflect:

The producers and writers of *24* consider Lynn McGill to be one of their highlights of the season. Executive producer Howard Gordon reveals, "He was a really tricky character. We're always looking for non-typical counterterrorist characters to populate CTU. Fellow co-executive producer David Fury continues, "We brought him in as a smart guy, a little green, who then became overwhelmed and started to become Commander Queeg [*The Caine Mutiny*] and gets to die a noble death. We gave him a heroic death, which I thought was great. It was a fantastic arc, one of the best arcs on the show."

In Memoriam: Tony Almeida

Career:

President, private security company
CTU – Special Agent in Charge, Los Angeles Domestic Unit
CTU – Deputy Director, Los Angeles Domestic Unit
Transmeta Corporation – Systems Validation Analyst

Expertise:

Certified Instructor, Krav Maga hand-to-hand combat
defense
Masters of Science, Computer Science, Stanford University
US Marines – First Lieutenant

Personal:

Spouse: Michelle Dessler (deceased)

Death:

Presumed murdered by lethal injection at approximately 7:59
pm, CTU Headquarters, Los Angeles Division

Tony Almeida R.I.P.

During *24*'s initial season, there was certainly no love lost between CTU Deputy Director Tony Almeida and Jack Bauer. Their management styles were oil and water with the sticking point of their shared former lover, Nina Myers, muddying the waters. Yet over the span of that incredibly long day surprisingly these men found a grudging respect for one another. Over the course of four more hellish days and the subsequent years, Tony and Jack became the staunchest friends and allies to the end. Tony Almeida proved himself to be an impressive man of action, second only to Jack, when he helped to bring down Peter Kingsley, and was responsible for saving the lives of both Teri Bauer and Audrey Raines. In his various leadership positions at CTU Almeida was more by-the-book than Jack ever was, but the two men were able to look beyond protocol and forge a great bond of trust that they both relied on in periods of extreme crisis. At times they physically clashed, with Tony taking one of Jack's bullets, but then Jack was there to get Tony out of prison and help guide him back on the path to CTU and the love of his life, Michelle Dessler. Tony Almeida was an inspiration despite his human flaws and a man that truly earned the mantle of hero.

Carlos Bernard Reflects:

As one of the few veterans of the cast to last five years, Carlos Bernard knew Tony Almeida's number would eventually come up. After helping to cover up Jack Bauer's death at the end of season four, the producers talked to Bernard about opening the next year with Tony's demise. "They came to me with the fifth season idea and were originally going to kill me with the bomb in the beginning, along with Michelle," Bernard reveals. "I said, 'I think it is a wasted opportunity and it would be much more interesting if he lives.' I don't mind dying on the show or not being on the show anymore. Frankly, for those of us who have been around since the first day, [the show] is like our baby and we want to be good to it. I don't want to be on there if it's going to be repetitive, if it's not going to contribute to the quality of the show. So I said, 'It would be cool if she dies, he lives, and he's on a rampage to find out who did it.' My idea was to find the guy who did it and try to kill him, but Jack still needed information from the guy, so Jack ends up having to kill Tony before he kills the guy. They loved the pitch I gave to them and were all for it.

"Well what ended up happening, and this is the thing about the show, is it is like a Rubik's Cube," Bernard explains. "All the parts, all the storylines, have to fit together time-wise, so you might have a great idea, but if it doesn't fit in with what is going on around it, you can't do it. What ended up happening with that idea is that it just didn't work; they had written themselves into a little bit of a corner by having me injured in the explosion. They had a real hard time working me back into it, so ultimately they ended up finding a way to kill me. I don't think any of us were crazy about how it happened; it just helped further the story. The story is the priority."

While Tony's anticlimactic death at the hands of Jack's former mentor, Christopher Henderson, might have packed less of an emotional punch than fans wanted, Bernard says his final day on the set was something he will always remember. "The last day of shooting they brought down this great cake to the CTU set and pretty much everyone involved with the show was there. It came down to just Kiefer and I who had been there throughout the whole series. On a personal level, it was very sad. They are such a great bunch of people and it's a great show. History will tell you you'll never be on something as big as that again. That's life and things come to an end."

The Producers Reflect:

Were there more stories to tell with Tony and Michelle? Co-executive producer David Fury says, "That's a good question and something that we struggled with. Unfortunately, with Tony it would have sent him into a revenge story, but revenge was Jack's story. Jack had lost Palmer and Michelle, and then later, Tony. If we had kept Tony alive, he would just be on the 'I want to get the people that killed Michelle' path. But that was exactly what Jack was doing, so we really struggled to figure out another angle to play with Tony and there just wasn't one. The only correct emotional place for him to be was revenge. Some people think that we should have let him be alive somewhere in a hospital. But sometimes a death is the more respectful way to get rid of a character, rather than just forget about them and let them fade away. While it was unfortunate that Tony didn't have a heroic moment [in death], he certainly had plenty in the course of the show." However, in the duplicitous world of 24 can you ever be certain someone has really died? Intriguingly the producers now refuse to confirm or deny Tony's death...

President
Charles Logan

Experience:

President of the United States
Lt. Governor of California
California State Congress, Representative (Santa Barbara)
Western Energy Coal & Reserve – CEO
Western Energy Coal & Reserve – Vice President
Pacific Nuclear Energy – Director

Education:

Princeton University – Bachelor of Arts, History

Honors:

Energy CEO of the Year

Personal:

Spouse – First Lady Martha Logan

Presidential Profile: Charles Logan

In the diverse pantheon of *24* villains, President Charles Logan stands very clearly as one of the most vile, deceptive and engaging enemies to ever square off against Jack Bauer. He may not have made his mark with double-barrels blazing or a killer Krav Maga kick, but he proved to be just as lethal an enemy with his talent for constantly turning the tables on Bauer throughout season five. Able to wriggle out of the most harrowing corners, Charles Logan had audiences seriously sweating that for once Bauer justice would not prevail, right up until the moment the crafty President was (thankfully) led away in disgrace as David Palmer's flag-draped casket provided somber witness.

For Tony-nominated character actor Greg Itzin, the wild and remarkable journey of Charles Logan, from weak Vice President to Machiavellian villain over two seasons, is one that not only took his career to new heights but allowed him to craft a character audiences consider a benchmark in *24* treachery. Back in season four, when Itzin was cast as President Keeler's second-in-command, the character was only supposed to be a means in credibly bringing the beloved David Palmer (Dennis Haysbert) back to the series. "When they hired me, they knew two things about the guy: that he was scared and that he had a hard time making a decision," Itzin offers. "I'm an actor and I get that totally! I plugged into that and it worked out well."

It worked in spades as Itzin's unctuous performance of a world leader clearly out of his element played so well that producers were smitten and determined that he would return the following season. Thrilled to get the chance to further explore Logan, Itzin says he came back with a very optimistic view of where the character could go. "In the fifth season, I thought he could be anything. I remember getting really excited because when I play the President of the United States or any character, I always try to make their motivations be positive. So in the opening episode we were doing this summit meeting with the Russians and me, and then David Palmer passed away, and I thought, 'This is great! Logan is going to get the chance to be a heroic President.' I always wanted my guy to be a hero.

"I remember Jude [Ciccolella] and I started the first couple of days of work and it was unformed. They had the scripts, but they didn't *have* the scripts. But the stances that we took reminded us — and we did it specifically — of the *Life Magazine* images of John F. Kennedy and RFK in the Oval Office with the sun streaming in. It was a beautiful memory, so we consciously mimicked those poses for ourselves and to also bring it up for people that lived in that period. Of course, shortly after that I became the weasel everybody loves to hate," Itzin laughs. "You don't know what's coming!"

While the producers admit they didn't know that Logan would eventually turn out to be the big villain of the year until midseason, they did know that Logan was going to be a much more complicated man, driven by ego and a marriage to Martha Logan that was clearly unraveling. Itzin says he focused immediately on that imploding relationship. "I've known Jean [Smart] for a long time," he explains. "As an actor, whenever you show up on a show for the first time you're trying to figure out how you fit in, so I talked to Jeanie right away. I said, 'We have a chance to do something really nifty here — to make this dysfunctional family real. We can make them something you don't see on TV and make them go to all kinds of places. They love each other and hate each other at the same time.' It worked for us from the very beginning, like in the scene where she comes out and tells me about David Palmer's death and I don't believe her conspiracy theory and say, 'I can't do this right now. Don't do this to me!'"

The actor says the couple's failed relationship just served to highlight Logan's own self-doubt and dismay at his fallen ideals. "Everybody that watches the show says to me, 'I hate you... but at the same time, I feel bad for you,' and that was exactly what I wanted," Itzin enthuses. "The guilt and self-loathing, his tantrums and his blame on other people are all just defense mechanisms for the great disdain that he held himself in. Martha had a line that she says to Novick like,

'What happened to him? When he started out he was the most idealistic man I ever knew.' I think it's important that you know that he started out as pure as the driven snow. I think it's a note on politics in general in that you don't know what you're getting into until you're in it, and then you find you have to compromise and compromise and compromise and pretty soon you aren't the person you started out to be. I gave a lot of thought to all of that stuff because I didn't want to have any false notes."

All of the care and thought put into Logan's motivations helped to bridge the producers' dark leap for the character — when it's revealed midseason that the President is the man behind the proverbial curtain, aiding the terrorists in order to secure US oil interests in Central Asia. Itzin says that when he was told the twist, sweat immediately poured out of him. "You know, I remember Kiefer saying to me around episode six that our characters at some later stage would be enemies. At a certain point, Howard Gordon also said that Logan couldn't continue to be the bumbling guy and it had to

go somewhere. About two episodes before the turn, with that great shot with me on the phone, they said, 'You are going to be found out to be complicit.' I said, 'Whoa? Wait, stop the presses here! I have to get my mind around this.' I didn't say 'No', but I did say, 'Huh?' I really had to go back and look at the episodes that had aired to find a pathway, so that I, Greg, as the character Logan, could believe that it was true. I had trouble with the death of Walt Cummings because when I was playing it in the moment and I said to him, 'How could you! You are a traitor...' I had to go back and look really hard at it to make myself believe and eventually, I just had to buy it that I had known at the time and I was backfilling like a mother," he laughs. "It just added another layer to his ability to be a bold-faced liar. What I really worked on was the thought that I can't just be a moustache-twirling villain. I can't be one-dimensional and this guy who is just a good liar. I thought, 'If I am going to place this, I have to be tormented,' and I think it added another dimension to him."

Pausing, Itzin then explains, "One of my favorite

actors is Robert Duvall. He was on one of those actor talks and he was speaking about when he really feels like he is 'on' and how you are always striving to be real, but, if you can't, you still have to act it! That's my creed. I try to make everything as real as possible. I'm blessed that I achieved that a lot of the time on 24. I just fell out and I was really in the moment a lot. I always asked myself, 'Can I get there? Can I get to that real place?' and I did time after time. So that's how I went down the road — everything that happened from a certain point tore Logan up inside. He had a sense of how he couldn't let the Presidency go down with him, so he had to cover. He became enmeshed in his own web, deeper and deeper."

Itzin says once he was able to give over to the story, the season became an embarrassment of riches to play.

"I was so lucky because in almost every episode there was something where I got to go, 'Oh God, I get to do that? That's so cool!'" he chuckles. "Like when he went to kill himself, I enjoyed that so much. First of all, it's just a great scene to do, and then the way they let it happen and the way they shot it — many people have remarked upon it. When they allowed me to walk out of Martha's door and do that whole long walk to my office — that was a gift. When I go to kill myself, he's really ready to do it because he really believes he deserves to be punished. It's also a coward's way out because then he doesn't have to face anything, but he's not thinking about that; he just wants the release."

But of course Logan doesn't go through with it and instead has to pay for his actions in two separate, gut-wrenching confrontations with Jack Bauer and then

Martha Logan in the final episode of the season. Itzin says, "I'm glad that [the Jack] showdown happened and then I got the showdown with my wife. In a way, what *24* needed was a showdown between Logan and Bauer, but Logan also needed to vent with the person that is most important in his life. That scene with Jeanie is the most satisfying because it's the most emotionally arresting for him; it's the most raw and open. Whereas with Jack he's devious and scared, but it's a different quality, without the same emotional involvement, because there is so much exposition and Kiefer did most of the talking. It was exhausting because the audience only sees it once, but we had to do it so many times. It was about trying to maneuver around what Jack says. But my favorite scene of the entire year is when I find out Martha has betrayed me. I take her in the hangar and both of us were running on all cylinders. We did the scene over and over and over again. Even though Jeanie was going through so much at the end of the day, we were elated. It's what we do best and we did it at the top of our game. I was glad that the

season built to that scene."

His fevered, relentless work as Charles Logan earned Itzin an Emmy nomination for Outstanding Supporting Actor in a Drama Series, and in turn, opened a wealth of new opportunities for the actor. "There's no character I've played onscreen better than Logan," he says frankly. "It was such a collaboration and I got so much screen time. I got to go everywhere emotionally. But the true gift is that I'm a journeyman actor; I've been acting a long time. Some people are familiar with my career and some people ask who I was before I was Logan, but I'm a character actor and a chameleon. I'm used to bringing my stuff to very complex roles on stage and there are theater parts that are on the same level as Logan. The gift was that I was allowed to do in front of a camera the kind of work that I've been doing for years on the stage. Hopefully playing Logan exposed me to a whole lot of people that can say, 'Come and play on my team.' I got to create this character through ties to me, I guess. I had real access to things as Logan and I miss him because I hardly ever get to play those parts."

First Lady
Martha Logan

Experience:

Santa Barbara Museum Board of Trustees
Southern California Shelters Fundraiser
Representative, Shine Walden Gallery

Education:

Stanford University – Bachelor of Arts, Art History

Personal:

Spouse – President Charles Logan

Presidential Profile: Martha Logan

When you have an actor like Greg Itzin crafting a character as distinctive and dastardly as Charles Logan, there's no question that it takes a thespian with equally sizable talents to match his onscreen chicanery beat for beat. In season five, when the *24* producers decided to introduce a spouse for Logan, they had no doubt as to whom the perfect actress would be to go against their weasely commander-in-chief — the incomparable Jean Smart.

For the last thirty years, the Emmy award-winning actress has made a lasting impression in the worlds of theater (*Lady Windermere's Fan*), film (*Garden State, Sweet Home Alabama*) and television (*Designing Women, Fraiser*). Equally adept at comedy and drama, Smart has played a rogues' gallery of diverse roles that run the gamut from fiery Southern hellcat to the most emotionally fragile of women. It was Smart's impressive range that led the producers to aggressively woo her to join the series to play Martha Logan — a role that earned her a much-deserved Emmy nomination for Outstanding Supporting Actress in a Drama Series.

In the able hands of Smart, Martha became a fascinating portrait of a woman at a crossroads in her life. Despite being fiercely intelligent and empathetic, Martha also suffered terribly due to her debilitating depression. Previously committed for a breakdown of unknown origins, the Martha Logan introduced to audiences with a shockingly dramatic dunk of her head into a bathroom basin full of water, was a woman literally at her emotional wits end. For Smart, the call to play a woman of such stature that was so damaged was hard to ignore. "I was definitely intrigued," she admits. "There's something about when someone asks you to play a First Lady. I met with [the producers] and liked them very much. It sounded like fun."

Yet having never seen the show, Smart says her first piece of business was getting caught up on the series by watching season four. "A big box of videotapes arrived at my door with all of season four," she remembers. "I watched it with my son, who was sixteen at the time, and we were addicted from the first tape. We sat down and started watching it in a marathon! We would have watched them all in three or four days but I felt like I would be a horrible mother if I let him, so he made me promise not to watch them while he was in school," she laughs. "It was really a remarkable season, so my only fear going into it was that people would say, 'Oh, season five was good but it's not what season four was.' And then I found out that Gregory Itzin was playing President Logan! We had worked together years before on stage. I adored him then and haven't worked with him since, and so I knew it would be fun. Greg didn't do a lot in season four, but he was brilliant. He looked like the proverbial deer caught in headlights playing that character," she chuckles. "So it was also a nice comfort level going into play such incredibly tense scenes with someone that I not only liked enormously, but also trusted as an actor."

While the producers admit their initial brainstorming for the Martha Logan character stemmed from Martha Mitchell, the larger-than-life wife of Nixon-era Attorney General John Mitchell, Smart says the character quickly veered away from that early model. "They told me about the character a little bit and basically what they told me, and this mutated in a lot of ways, is that before it was cast they were thinking about someone that was a loose cannon and so they looked to Martha Mitchell. But ultimately the only thing they kept from that idea was the name, because I don't think of my character as anything remotely like Martha Mitchell. My memory of Martha Mitchell is this woman with a big smile and big beehive. I guess she was a bit of a loud mouth and a loose cannon, but I don't know how much of that was her personality or just political spin."

In fleshing out Martha, Smart says she focused on her depression, which became the defining undercurrent to all of the character's motivations, whether she was manic or lucid. "I think that a lot of people

that suffer from forms of depression are often extremely capable and intelligent," Smart explains. "They have more of a radar than some people and they take in everything. They take everything too much to heart and worry too much. I saw her as someone who in some ways is perfect for the position [of First Lady]; but in other ways, it was the worse thing in the world for her, because of the complete lack of privacy and not being allowed to be herself. I can't think of a worse job that any woman would be thrust into — except for some of the perks," she asides with a smile, "— than being the First Lady of the United States. And to think that it might go on for years and years and years, I can't imagine anyone wouldn't lose their mind!"

Smart also clearly imagines that a life in the global spotlight helped to destroy the Logan marriage. "The thing about the Logans is that most of the time we were seeing them behind the scenes, and we rarely get to see our politicians that way. We got a lot of freedom to see them as human beings, which they are. But you rarely saw Martha in her professional capacity and she probably handled that fairly well, though she might have called in sick a few more times than she should have," Smart grins. "So we didn't get to see that side to her very much, but we saw the anger and the vulnerability." The actress says she and Itzin worked to create a back-story that helped fill in the blanks to their disintegration. This strengthened the story that audiences didn't see but certainly felt every time the couple was on screen. "We figured they met when she was in Grad school and he was a young state representative. I think they were very much in love and a pretty good team. I think they were young and idealistic and the fact that he went the way that he eventually went was the thing that really hurt her the most. He gave up on the idealism and became the bad guy in her eyes. Not only did he turn from her but also he turned to the dark side. When she became disillusioned with her husband, that was the straw that broke that camel's back."

Thus the writers and Smart were in accord in playing Martha as a woman on the verge, as evidenced in her jaw-dropping introduction when a disdainful assessment of her "wedding cake" appearance in the mirror causes her to dunk her head in water so she can start again. "It's my favorite introduction of any character I've ever played," Smart laughs with glee. "It was written like that and when I read it, I said, 'I've got to play this character!' I thought it was a

brilliant piece of writing. It's so startling and says more about Martha in a matter of seconds than I ever could have said in pages of dialogue. It spoke about her impulsivity, that she did it so calmly. But on the very first day when I arrived on the set, they said they were thinking about cutting it out! My knees about buckled and I did a lot of fast talking and begging to convince them not to. They were being practical because they said it would take hours between each take to redo the makeup and hair and costume. But I got together with the fabulous hair and makeup people and we convinced them we could do it in two takes. We had an extra wig all set and we actually did it in one take!"

As disturbing as that scene was, Smart also says it showed another side of Martha that she clung to throughout the season. "I love that it spoke to the

weird sense of humor that Martha has, which I think got confused very often. I always thought of her having this quirky sense of humor, like in the scene where she's locked in her room and there's this big, burly secret service agent outside her door. She is asking him some questions and he's very mono-syllabic and she says, 'You don't have much of a personality, do you?'

"Or the scene with the poor young man that she walks in on in the men's room when she was trying to get the key from him. That was my favorite scene!" she enthuses. "He was brilliant because he was trying so hard to match her level of business, but he's caught literally with his pants down. He's so mortified and just trying to answer her questions. And then she buttons her blouse back up and it's done."

The actress says the writers also allowed a very

different facet of Martha to bloom over the season through her interactions with Agent Aaron Pierce. Their quiet, unrequited connection brought a positive vulnerability to Martha that audiences loved. "I wasn't sure about it initially, because I didn't know what [the producers] had in mind, but I grew to be very fond of that idea," Smart admits. "And Glenn Morshower is such a wonderful actor and person. I used to call him my big boy scout because his character was very much by the book and no matter how he felt, he would never step over that line, which was adorable. Unfortunately, the scene where you first realize that he has feelings for her and she's startled when she finds out was cut. It was the very first time you caught a glimpse that he cares for her and she's speechless. Later, she asks him to come to her room and thanks him for saving her life, but that followed the scene where he initially said something to her. I think she was so hungry for that and she went into it as well and let her feelings go [to him]. I used to kid that when your husband tries to blow you up in a limousine and another man saves your life, it tends to color your opinion," she laughs.

Yet it was the incredibly dysfunctional dynamic between Martha and Charles that had audiences and critics enthralled all season. "I think Gregory and I both knew it was something special," Smart reflects. "Of course, when people respond and agree and you

get kudos for it, then that's incredibly nice and it felt really great. I can't say enough good things about Gregory. I'd see the look in his eyes where he's there every second giving you whatever you need, and that makes such a difference. I thought it was great. In the middle of season five we both were hoping we'd make it to the end, but we had no idea. Then when we found out not only were we going to make it to the end of the season, but also that the finale was about us, that was really flattering and fun."

While the actress was disappointed that she and Itzin didn't win the Emmys for their roles, Smart says her true satisfaction lies in the legacy that the characters will forever leave on the series. "I was very pleased and I think that it was a satisfying arc. It was a good ending to the characters and satisfying for the show and for us as actors. And as far as acting on camera, I would say Martha is more along the lines of some of the characters I've played on stage. I've had the chance to play some of the great women's roles in literature and it's rare to find in television or film a female role that is more than utilitarian, so she was extremely satisfying and I'm really glad I got to do it."

Outstanding Drama Series

It took five *long* years, and to tell the truth, most people at *24* had really given up on the idea of ever winning an Emmy for Outstanding Drama Series, despite being nominated every year since the series began. In Hollywood, a series in its fifth year that hasn't won a Best Drama Emmy before has a very rare shot of ever getting one. That distinction usually goes to standout freshman hits, like *Lost*, or shows that become multiple-year Emmy dynasties like *The Sopranos*. But in August 2006, the impossible happened when *24* finally got its coveted win, taking home the statue on behalf of all the producers, writers, cast and crew that have pretty much stayed with the series since the pilot.

Reflecting on that night and what winning the Emmy means to the show overall, the producers share their thoughts:

Executive producer Howard Gordon smiles when he thinks back on that August evening because he didn't think they had a shot in hell of winning. "No chance," he says frankly. "So it was stunning and a complete surprise. I've always been kind of down on these things. I've been nominated eight or nine times, for *The X-Files* and *Beauty and the Beast*, so at some point you start making rationalizations, like, 'It doesn't matter' and 'Who cares!' But having won, it's clearly a very wise and sage process and a great group of people who vote," he jokes. "It really felt good. It was a real approbation on so many levels. I think there was an awful lot of goodwill."

Producer and director Brad Turner says as the fifth season was in production he didn't get a sense that the year was going to be more special than previous years. "I think overall, we don't know if we are hitting on all cylinders until a season is over. Regardless, we are bold enough to throw pretty radical ideas out there and see how they fly. We live on the praise and also the criticism. I don't think that anyone is saying we are losing originality, and believe me, trying to create this year after year... people were telling us we couldn't do it for one year, let alone six years! So I don't think year five was any different in terms of going into it, but I think you have to bring up the ideas of movies and talk about chemistry. It's very hard to connect the dots with chemistry but sometimes you get all the right people in the right places at the right time. It's like trying to produce six hit movies in a row with the same scenario. People look at our show as a twenty-four-hour movie, and I think it's criticized on that level unfairly, because there's no way to do that perfectly. Season five just had strong scenarios that surprised us."

Turner says he hopes the award also signifies the body of work generated on *24*. "I think we kind of earned [the Emmy] through the rest of the seasons. I believe we worked our way up to it and the Academy was looking for the year that was really exceptional. Five happened to be the right year. We were nominated every year because it's an impossible show to do and people in the business realize how impossible it is. That's why we kept getting nominated right up to year five and I think it was also an opportunity to recognize great effort in the fifth year."

Fellow director and co-executive producer Jon Cassar says he still thinks back on Emmy night as a pretty magical moment in time for the show. "It's really interesting because I don't think there has been another night in my life more exciting than that. I think the key was that we all won. Winning that award by myself, and most people won't believe me when I say it, but if Kiefer didn't win that night and all the other producers didn't have one in their hands, it wouldn't have been the same. There is no way winning that award by myself would have even started to touch how happy I was that we all got it together. I

was the first one to win out of everybody, and my wife looked at me and said, 'Dude, you just won an Emmy. Look at your face?' And I said, 'Yeah, but Kiefer's is coming up and if he doesn't win it, then it's not the same. I won this because of him.' Then I looked back at the producers and thought, 'If they don't win it, then it's not the same either.' I am so happy they gave it to us as a team. I won the DGA Award four months later and that singled me out, and I'm not comfortable in that place. As much as it was great to win, it wasn't like winning the Emmy with Kiefer and all my boys. I really felt like it was a family night and all that hard work we put in for years together finally paid off. People don't realize that it's been our fifth year and every year we heard *Lost* and other shows but not us," he laughs. "After the third or fourth year, you figure there won't be a next year because shows in their fifth year don't win Emmys. We made peace with the fact that we were proud of the show we were making and we weren't

going to be the show to win awards. It's funny that the year we made peace with it, we won. The stars aligned and it's all good."

Cassar continues, "The funny part is the press was asking, 'What are you going to do now? Are you going to take some time off?' This isn't the Academy Awards, where people make a movie and four months later they get an award. I was working the next day! I said, 'Look around. Ninety percent of the people here have a 6.00 am call tomorrow morning. This is the world of television — you just keep going! Luckily, I didn't have a morning call, but that night I went and blew up the bus from the first episode [of season six]. I was in downtown LA, doing the very first scene of the next year. It was oddly fitting that I won for the previous year opener and that next night I was blowing up a bus. The wheel kept on moving!"

Actor and executive producer Kiefer Sutherland says he also cherished his personal win more because the rest of the *24* team was singled out too. "Jon was my favorite part of the night. He works so hard and no one knows that except for us and if anyone deserved that night, it was him. It was special to be able to stand there with your friends that you've worked with for five years. Most things, whether it's a show or a restaurant, don't ascend through five years. They hit their flash mark and then start to descend. It's something we have all been hyper-sensitive about, that this is one of those great opportunities in a lifetime and it's not something to be taken lightly or for granted. We have had a lot of support from our fans along the way and that's not to be taken lightly either. We will go to great lengths to make sure we don't get lazy with it. So to be honored like that in a fifth year, it's certainly nothing that we would have ever imagined, so it was a special night."

For co-creator and executive producer Robert Cochran, winning for the fifth season was particularly special because he felt it was the show's best season. "Having been nominated a number of times before, we thought there was a reasonable chance we would get nominated for it and if we did, this is a worthy season. I'm not saying we thought we would win, because you would be crazy to think that, but we really thought this was our best season and we had as good a chance as we ever had [to win it]. We were still thrilled and surprised when it happened, but nevertheless, we all thought this season was our best shot."

Cochran also appreciates that the show was honored for being different and trying something nobody thought could be done on TV — a real-time format. "It makes us feel good that we actually are doing something that has never been done before. We always felt a little pride about that. We joke that it's hard to do and God knows we've had our desperate moments, but we've been able to keep it on the air. Five straight Emmy nominations for a format that is truly different is a very special feeling."

In his irrepressibly frank way, co-creator and executive producer Joel Surnow says awards are never on his radar. "With this show you're in a hypnotic state for nine months, you really are. Every now and then you come up for air and you get nominated for something and it's great. You celebrate it for half a

day and then you're back into the muddle. But we celebrate every little victory we get, whether it's a ratings victory or something else, we take the time to go light up a cigar in the smoke room and savor it."

He continues, "We also savor the idea that we are still excited and inspired to do the show after five years. It sounds cheesy but that is the reward. The accolades are great and we love them, but they wouldn't mean anything if we didn't think we were still doing really good work. We did feel like we earned it and that we put out a really entertaining season, as good as any of the previous four seasons. I don't think the show has taken a quality dip in five years. I think there are always episodes or arcs that work or don't work, but it's the same writers, directors and crew at the same level of commitment. We just feel good when we pick up a thread of a story that we think can work. Believe it or not, that is the thing that gets us most excited. I think the awards and all that will mean more when we are off the show and we don't have anything else to talk about. Right now, we are too busy doing it."

Outstanding Director for a Drama

If there's something that fans have come to expect of *24* it's that the opening episodes of the season are nail-biting extravaganzas that set the tone for the new day. Every year since the second season, director **Jon Cassar** has been the man entrusted to helm those pivotal starter episodes that also serve to tempt new viewers into trying out Jack Bauer's world. Cassar's particular strength of balancing character dynamics with action stems from his unique background as a skilled, action cameraman for film. After many years, he transitioned to directing episodic television shows such as, *Forever Knight, Due South, Kung Fu: The Legend Continues* and *Profiler*. Since joining *24*, Cassar has been able to marry his rare abilities of being both an actor's director and a top-notch visual director to help infuse the series with a sense of depth and urgency that connects with viewers. Cassar's singular talents were finally recognized in 2006 when he was awarded the Emmy for Outstanding Director for the fifth season première of *24*.

Season five's particularly tricky opener required Jon to find the right tone and balance as several major storylines needed to be addressed immediately in a short period of time. "For me as a director, I have to make sure that we hit the ground running," Cassar explains. "I need a story that is strong enough and I have a visual sense of story that is going to drive people right away. This particular episode was one of the best episodes I've ever done. I can say that because I won a whole bunch of awards for it: an Emmy and a DGA award," he smiles. "But it was also one of the hardest shows I've ever done because the first shows are always the hardest. There is a sense of unease; it's new ground — like a pilot. Everyone is questioning everything you are doing and it becomes a battle to make sure we get everything right. The thing about *24* is that every year, we are starting from scratch again. We — the writers, the directors and the actors — are very concerned about how we kick off a new season. It's got to be as perfect as we think we can make it in the time we have. Kiefer is a huge spearhead with that. He knows how important that first show is, so he's a big part of that, as are Joel Surnow, Howard Gordon, Bob Cochran, Evan Katz... all of them. It's always a main concern, introducing new characters and new sets. The word 'new' becomes very important — as well as not doing it in a way that makes your audience disappear. We want to introduce new people and new storylines to an audience that is very loyal, but we don't want to alienate them — that's always my main concern."

First off in this particular episode, Cassar and company had to resurrect Jack Bauer from his self-imposed "death". Cassar remembers, "In this case, we made such an effort to make Jack go away that it needed to be something huge to pull him back. We painted ourselves a little bit into a corner at the end of the year by saying Jack is dead and he's walking down the highway, because then you go, 'Uh oh! Now we have to bring him back!'"

So what better way to force Jack into action than to kill the people that mean the most to him? With the murder of David Palmer, Michelle Dessler and the wounding of Tony Almeida, there were suddenly three very good reasons to have Bauer back in the picture. "Nobody knew where Jack was, but the fact that his friends are being killed was enough to pull him back in," Cassar explains. "Palmer, Tony and Michelle are his best friends so that's going to affect him for the rest of the year. The key to the season is making sure Jack Bauer has a drive every year; he is the hardest one to write. Everyone else can react to the moment; Jack instinctively reacts to the moment and he's the superman of fighting terrorism, but if that was all he did you wouldn't watch the show. It would get boring really quickly if all he did was be Jack Bauer — terrorist fighter. You watch the show because he is Jack Bauer — human being. It's always about what is the line that will drive Jack, and for year five, it was all those things coming together."

As compelling as those deaths were to Jack's seasonal

motivation, it also left Cassar with the very difficult process of visualizing their deaths properly, both within the scenes and in the context of the overall episode. "My concern was, because we were eliminating characters that had been with us for so long, I wanted to make sure their endings did justice to their characters. We had to make them go out in a way that was respectful of them and of their characters and not alienate the audience — although of course we were going to alienate the audience," he says candidly. "These are well loved characters, so emotionally we were going to scar the audience. But when people ask why we killed these

characters — was it just going for the sensational kill? I say, 'No, it was not!' We do it because of the way it affects Jack or Chloe or the people at CTU.

"And it was a matter of, 'Can we write Dennis Haysbert being Palmer yet again? And the same for Tony and Michelle?' As for the actors, not that they wanted to leave, but if all they see on the horizon is the same thing, they are kind of glad to go too. Carlos Bernard and Reiko Aylesworth felt that way, but maybe Dennis, not as much," Cassar concedes. "I think he really enjoyed playing the President and he did a great job, but we didn't want to get repetitious. When fans ask me: 'Why did you do it?' or 'How dare you?' I say, 'Well look, if we didn't kill those first characters like Teri Bauer, you wouldn't have Chloe, Edgar or even Michelle. She came in when we moved people out from the first year and that's the evolution of the show."

Aside from the Bauer story complexities, Cassar says that episode provided a myriad of other difficulties that were his responsibility to overcome. "On the first day I had a whole new set to deal with — the retreat," he remembers. "It was a beautiful set designed by Joseph Hodges, but incredibly difficult from a lighting and shooting standpoint, just because it was new. But it all worked out pretty well and it wasn't as scary as I thought it would be. We also had some problems with a bad guy that wasn't quite right so we had to change the actors three times, which meant going back and re-shooting," he sighs.

Season five also offered the introduction of a brand-new White House storyline that was heavily mired in the personal drama between Charles and Martha Logan. "The Washington side was very new," Cassar explains. "We had Greg Itzin the year before with a small arc, but now I was in charge of dealing with a whole new administration with Charles and Martha. It was very difficult because I had to introduce this new wife, who is not stable, so I had to deal with that as a director, and keep it all in the realm of reality for us. It was very, very sensitive material to pull off, but with Jean Smart and I working together, it was a dream!" In particular, he references the scene where the audience first meets Martha and she dunks her head in the sink. Laughing, Cassar says, "[Jean] loved that this woman goes down to this level, but playing all of those things was the next most challenging thing for me. Right off

the bat, you had to know who all these people were — Charles, Martha and their relationship. But I was blessed with some of the most incredible actors, and once I started doing those scenes, I felt we had a great foundation for a good year, knowing that their storyline was so strong. For me, I just believed that if I could pull it off, their story and the Jack storyline were both going to be really strong."

Proud of the success of the episode and the other Emmy wins for season five, Cassar says, as corny as it may sound, his true reward is working with the *24* family. "The hardest thing in this business is to find a group of people that you love and that you work with really well and do good work with. I've worked on shows where you love everybody, but the material sucks," he laughs. "On this show we have both. We are the lucky, lucky show with the greatest people to work with and really good work to do. If we stay together forever, we are happy with that because we are doing great work and we get to smile everyday. Looking at *24*, I think the greatest gift to me has been the ability to do what I really want to do and the opportunity these guys have given me to do it. I'm going to look back on this and know I did the best work of my life because I have producers that believe in me and that stayed out of my way to let me do what I do. I can look back proudly on every show."

Outstanding Single-Camera Picture Editing for a Drama Series

Deep within the *24* office building, there's a room of darkened suites in the far corner where the outside light never comes inside. It's the domain of the *24* editors where sunshine is supplanted by the glow of their AVID computer monitors, illuminating the team feverishly cutting together Jack Bauer's latest violent adventures. There are always three full-time *24* editors; some have come and gone over the years, but their talents have earned the series five American Cinema Editor award nominations and ten Emmy award nominations. For his impressive work on the season five première, editor **David Latham** won the Emmy for Outstanding Single-Camera Picture Editing for a Drama Series for the episode '7:00 am - 8:00 am'.

It was Latham's first Emmy win in his twenty-plus year career editing a broad range of classic TV shows. With his ever-present smile and cheerful demeanor, Latham is humble about his achievements. He explains he's been working in edit rooms his whole life. "I was an assistant editor for a long time, but then the first show I started editing for was *The A-Team* twenty years ago. I was at Universal for eight years and then went to Stephen J. Cannell Productions for eight years where I did *Hunter* and *21 Jump Street* — I was very proud of *Jump Street*. Then I went and edited *Baywatch*," he chuckles with a coy smile. "After that I did *Walker Texas Ranger* and then I got lucky over here." Latham tossed his hat in the *24* editorial ring in 2001, and says he was surprised at the results. "Normally anybody would have looked at my resumé and said, '[*Pfft*] Loser!' But I met Joel Surnow and made a couple of jokes with him, and the next day he said, 'Come on out here. You're hired.' I was stunned. He said he noticed on my resumé that wherever I was, I stayed, so it meant I knew what I was doing," Latham laughs heartily.

Asked if there is a key to his editorial talents, Latham is a bit stumped until he offers, "I love puzzles! I do a couple of crossword puzzles every day." While that may seem random, it actually perfectly describes an editor's job. They are tasked with putting together the miles of footage filmed for every episode, creating a semblance of order to all the material that comes into an editing station in disjointed pieces. The episodes aren't shot according to the flow of the script, so the sequences that come in are like pieces of a very large moving-image puzzle that needs to eventually coalesce into a well-paced story, consisting of forty-three minutes, six seconds and eight frames. A challenge that Latham says is right up his alley: "I am a visually-oriented person and editing is like assembling puzzles. When I go through the film, I see the pieces that have impact and great movement or performance, and one way or another I'm going to get that into a scene. Even if it's not the strongest take or it doesn't lead to the next piece very well, I'm going to find a way to make all these pieces fit and get all the best pieces in somehow, and make it all fluid. You move things around and make it work."

An editor from the very beginning, Latham says, as you would expect, the real-time format was the biggest learning curve. "There are no time cuts and you move the story along by moving people from here to here to here. When someone is driving across town, we have to put them in a car for forty-five minutes; they can't just show up. I just have to get people across a room when it's not very exciting."

What Latham and his fellow *24* editors have done is create their own particular bag of visual tricks to make the show work. "You have to cheat with some cuts that

speed it up, without it being obvious that you've jumped them ahead. We move scenes around and that helps us out a lot when things get boring. We can take some chunks out or if it's too obvious to get around, we can move the scenes. The boxes help a lot too. Instead of holding while someone walks across a room, you can go to a box and you make people look at it with a fresh perspective. It also moves someone along, maybe even ten to fifteen steps, which helps a lot!"

Over the five seasons, the editing style of the show has changed too. Cuts are faster, with about one thousand per episode (including music, effects and more). Latham says the intense style suits him. "The pacing hasn't been difficult for me, I love it. I've always liked fast movement in film and it fits what I've always done real well. I'm not sure if it's partially because of the way I always did things that the show looks like this. I started at the beginning, so me and the other editors have dictated what it looks like."

The average time to edit an episode varies vastly depending on where they are in the production season. But Latham says the process remains the same from episode to episode. "I have the first cut put together the day after they finish shooting. I keep up as they shoot. Whenever I get a scene that has completed shooting, I

cut the whole thing and add the sound effects and the music. Each scene is separate and has its own little tone. The last day of shooting is usually just one piece of a sequence that is going to have to be massively boxed and fit into the whole."

After the first cut is done, Latham continues, "The director comes in. For the opening episode it was Jon Cassar. We usually see eye-to-eye on so many things that he'll maybe have a couple changes to a show. A part of editing is reading a director's mind; when you're looking at the film you're going, 'Okay, he did this for some reason, but what is it? Where does he want it?' Then I'll figure it out," he smiles. "I've worked with him for a long time so I can usually figure out what he's going for. When Jon's happy with it, [co-executive producer] Stephen Kronish comes in and will look at it. First off, we have a ton of laughs and enjoy ourselves all day. We'll make jokes and start taking some lines out to move it along better. Maybe we'll shuffle a couple of scenes around and add some lines and that's pretty much it. All of that takes about a day. He might look at it again and then we'll wait until Joel Surnow takes a look. Sometimes a show will sit here for three weeks, so my assistants will be working on the visual effects. Otherwise, we wait until Joel signs off on it and then I go up and watch the audio mix and that's it. We also send it to the studio and the network who usually have little notes. They are the last ones to look at it before we lock it."

Unlike other shows, Latham says the editors at *24* have a lot of freedom to shape the episodes. "They leave us be for the process. No one comes in and looks at scenes while they are being cut, unless I alert them about something not working. Otherwise they expect and want me to take lines out, add lines, move scenes around and do all these things that a producer normally does on the first pass. They expect us to make a producers' pass. I love working with Joel, he said at the beginning, 'Put your stink on it,'" Latham laughs.

Looking back specifically on season five's '7:00 am - 8:00 am', Latham says, "I was surprised it won because that first show was so long and we had to take so much out. We ended up taking a lot of lines out and people jump all over the place, and that's really tricky to do without it being very obvious. You have to go to close-ups, change looks, but fortunately [the cameramen] are

always crossing what they call 'the line', which refers to the eye lines and how people are looking at each other. When you do that on a regular basis you can kind of confuse people as to where people are, by where they are looking — I notice it though!" he chuckles.

Latham says there were other issues in the episode too. "I think Joel showed the show to some people and came back in and said it was too slow and we needed to pick up the pace. For instance, with Michelle and Tony's scene, we took out a whole bunch of lines and a lot of moving around, so I was pleased with that in the end. I also like the opening sequence with the boxes and Jack at the oilrig. But I wasn't crazy about the helicopter blowing the smoke around for the gun battle. Not to mention the fact that we had three different bad guys in that show because we kept changing them! One guy ran out and started to do a chase and messed up his leg, and so we were going to make him the assistant bad guy and promoted another bad guy. We went back and re-shot things, but that guy wasn't very good. Then we went out and hired another guy to be the new bad guy, and we filmed him being killed

at the end. But they didn't like it, so we tossed it and got another guy and did it again! The way they wrote it, Jack kills this guy who confessed to being behind the Palmer assassination. They wanted to push into the final boxes, like we usually do, before we even got to that scene. I knew it was going to be a very long scene at the end. We usually like to come back for a small piece that is a grabber, so I suggested to Joel that we move into the boxes right when Jack hears that this guy killed Palmer. Then we come back out and the guy says, 'Take me to the hospital' and Jack stands up and kills him. It made it a much more succinct ending, instead of playing a two-and-half-minute scene after our final boxes. They liked it a lot and that was my idea."

Now an Emmy winner, Latham just laughs at the new title. While he's proud of his work, he says the greatest reward is still being part of the *24* team. "I just love it here! I never want it to end. I want it to get to the point where it's the twentieth year and we are watching people sleep because we can't figure out what to do anymore!"

Outstanding Music Composition for a Series

From the instantly recognizable theme to the most subtle underscore played behind a particularly tense scene, the score of *24* originates from the musical mind of composer **Sean Callery**. The maestro behind the soundtrack of the series since the pilot, Callery has infused Jack Bauer's world with his unique audible point of view for five years. His eclectic exploration of musical genres and styles has created unifying themes for entire seasons, while heightening the drama and emotional resonance in more than 120 episodes. Try to imagine an episode of *24* without Callery's compositions adding just the right punch to an action scene or providing the grace note for an intense character exchange, and the silence left is truly deafening. Callery's work has earned him five Emmy nominations and two wins for Outstanding Music Composition For a Series, including his work on the fifth season finale, '6:00 am - 7:00 am'.

At the beginning of season five, Callery says he began, as he usually does, by setting up the overall feel for the year. "I always consult with Jon Cassar and Joel Surnow in terms of style and color and the themes of the overall season. Season five was one of the years where music was needed everywhere. It was participating almost as a background character. Like in the interrogation scenes, when you are sitting in a room uncomfortably, musically something might be able to be done, almost subconsciously, to give that unsettling feeling. So there was a lot of tremendous stuff planted at the beginning of season five and it just grew organically from there and I'm happy to say it worked out really well for everybody."

Upon reading the first script of the season and watching the edit of the episode, Callery says that he was able to find the season's overall tone based on two important events. "One of the principle tasks in episode one was to get Jack Bauer back in the game. The other thing was to deal with Palmer's death, so there is a feeling of shock. When you have a national tragedy, it's everywhere. Joel is very good at using words like, 'You can feel the tension and the sadness in the air.' That's a lot for a composer to chew on in terms of what you would do if you had to make a sound for a national sense of mourning. I certainly didn't go into my bag of tricks and say, 'Here are the colors for mourning a dead President.' You have to discover those things and that's what I try to do with each show.

"It was a very powerful opening," Callery continues. "In the first few minutes, we had to say goodbye to a major character. I don't think there has been a season beginning that was as emotional. Normally at the beginning of the season there is a very serious event or a terrorist-related activity, but this was more complex. It was a tragic, evil event and a beloved character, on the spot, went away. I'm a fan as well as an employee of the show, so I was very moved by it. We had some themes for President Palmer that we were able to sort of, if you will, celebrate one final time. It started to unfold at the very beginning of the season and I'm happy to say it continued right to the end with the celebration of his coffin."

Callery says another great source of musical inspiration for him in season five was the fine work of the cast. "The other thing that was particularly powerful for me was that I just loved the characters of President Logan and Martha Logan. They were so fabulous. Greg and Jean's presence on the show

brought even more musical opportunity. It brought a different color because the B-story was just as powerful as the A-story. Years ago I studied acting just to learn how scenes are put together. I found with the really blessed actors there is so much going on, even when they are not speaking, in every single moment. I really felt that in season five from Kiefer on down, including Greg and Jean, you saw that everywhere. When that kind of acting is going on, it makes a job like mine easier because you are just looking at the picture and getting out of the way."

Each character gets their own theme, from Jack Bauer down to Chloe, which gets repeated throughout a season to underscore their emotional beats. "If I do my job right, the music grows with the character, it should never get ahead of the story or drag it down." One of Callery's favorite music cues in season five was for Martha Logan. "In the very first scene that you see Jean Smart, she dunks her head into a sink," the composer laughs. "So much is there already that even without music and her just looking into the mirror the viewer can tell that she hasn't got it all together. I even asked Joel about how loony we wanted to make [her music]. I think I developed one unique little sound for her. Whenever she went crazy, this violin came in every now and again as she was teetering on

the brink. I used it very sparingly but I got letters from fans saying it was very cool. So it was sort of a signature for her at times."

Martha's theme intertwines with that of Charles Logan's, providing more fertile musical ground for Callery. "Later on in the season their marriage became very estranged. It was surreal in a way, like there was no life between them, yet they were together. It was like a no man's land. I remember the scene where Logan almost kills himself. He says he's sorry to her and she says she doesn't care. It was a moment of utter despair and sadness. There is so much pain between them, which I underscored."

In Callery's Emmy-winning episode, the composer says he loved the fact that he got to add his musical touch to the climax of the season. "My favorite scene in episode '6.00 am – 7.00 am' is the one where Logan falls. If you remember that act, it begins with Logan walking past the coffin and he thinks he is out of the woods. He gives this very moving speech about Palmer, but juxtaposed with that is CTU, where they are playing back the secret recording of Martha Logan that exposes Logan. If you study the scene, they shoot Logan from the bleachers and the camera is very slowly zooming in on him and then it cuts back to hearing Charles and Martha screaming at each other. The whole undercurrent of the scene is one of heartbreak. I had to really pay attention to what I was feeling when I was watching it, and the truth of it is that I was sad. You spend the whole season chasing this corrupt President and finally everybody is hearing just how horrible he is. You can see it in the faces of the actors and in Jon's direction. For me it was heartbreaking, so the score from the very beginning of the speech to his arrest is akin to if you have a goal and you reach it, there is a feeling of great accomplishment but also a feeling of sadness that the journey is over. Logan is then arrested and he walks to his car while Palmer's coffin is being put on the plane. It's a great moment because the corrupt President is being taken into custody while you are fully celebrating the life of a character that was on the show for five years. It was so spectacularly directed and acted.

"One of the challenges we face on a show like this is finding a sense of resolution. Throughout the

show's twenty-four episodes, there have to be peaks and valleys. There has to be tension and the release of tension in order to keep going, otherwise people would have heart attacks! The last episode really has to deliver and I have to say that of all the seasons, I thought '6.00 am – 7.00 am' was the most complete in terms of emotion, action, suspense, character, drama, the whole thing. It's a superb climax!"

An important part of that satisfaction with the finale came from Callery's musical contributions, which the Academy of Television Arts and Sciences duly recognized with his Emmy win. Callery offers, "I have to say that I've never taken for granted being nominated – ever. Being nominated is an honor. I know it sounds cliché, but there are so many composers out there writing so much good music. To be nominated was amazing and to win, it does blow your mind a little bit. You feel immensely humbled. I was nominated in both instances with collectively eight other talented composers. I think what was particularly sweet about season five was that I got to

go to the main telecast. I remember when Greg and Jean didn't prevail, I had this sinking feeling, I thought to myself, 'If we weren't able to win this year, then we aren't meant to ever.' But then Jon won for direction and Kiefer won for best actor. It was one of those moments when it almost all comes together, with the exception of Jean and Greg. But when they were announcing the Emmy for best series, I was in the balcony and I decided to go downstairs because there was a feeling it was going to happen. We were excited but we didn't think it was *definitely* going to happen. I guess I was confident enough to get out of my seat and go down to the front. When they announced *24*, so many people from the cast and crew went up on stage. I thought it was totally appropriate because everyone works so hard on the show. I've never worked on a show that has this much cohesion in terms of respect and good will. It works from the top down, with Joel, Bob, Howard and Jon. It keeps people together and makes you always want to strive to do your best."

INTO SEASON SIX